MOTORCYCLE *classics*

BY DOUG MITCHEL AND THE
AUTO EDITORS OF CONSUMER GUIDE®

Publications International, Ltd.

Louis Weber, C.E.O.
Publications International, Ltd.
7373 North Cicero Avenue
Lincolnwood, Illinois 60646

Permission is never granted for commercial purposes.

Manufactured in U.S.A.

8 7 6 5 4 3 2 1

ISBN: 0–7853–0889–X

Library of Congress Catalog Card Number:
94-74830

Dedication

In addition to all of the motorcycle owners listed within these pages, I would like to extend a special thanks to those who went above and beyond the call of duty and helped to make this book possible:

Pete and Joey Bollenbach and the Bollenbach Engineering team for their tireless patience and numerous contacts in the world of motorcycling.

Dave Kiesow, Bob Maxant, and Tim Farrel at Illinois Harley-Davidson for their constant assistance with both motorcycles and information.

The entire Kersting family for making me feel at home on my numerous visits to Kersting's Harley-Davidson.

Dick Cogswell, Jerry Mannino, and Matt Yingling at Laurel BMW for tolerating my repeated visits to their showroom without buying a single thing.

Bob Nowak from the Chicago Norton Owners Club for introducing me to the world of British cycles and their owners.

Paul Pfaffle and the crew at Vintage Classics for steering me toward several rare finds.

My family and friends for their undying support and for listening to all of my boring motorcycle stories.

And last, but not least, to all of my fellow enthusiasts across the globe who share my all-consuming passion for the sport of motorcycling.

UNITED STATES   GERMANY   ITALY   JAPAN   GREAT BRITAIN

CONTENTS

UNITED STATES

GERMANY

ITALY

JAPAN

GREAT BRITAIN

1948 Indian Chief (U.S.)   **64**

1949 Harley-Davidson FL (U.S.)   **66**

1951 Triumph T100 (Great Britain)   **68**

1951 Vincent HRD Series B Rapide (Great Britain)   **70**

1952 Triumph Thunderbird (Great Britain)   **72**

1953 Indian Chief (U.S.)   **74**

1953 Triumph Drag Bike (Great Britain)   **76**

1954 AJS 16M (Great Britain)   **78**

1954 Harley-Davidson FLF (U.S.)   **80**

1956 Simplex Automatic (U.S.)   **82**

1957 Ariel 4G Mk II (Great Britain)   **84**

1959 Ariel Leader (Great Britain)   **86**

1959 Harley-Davidson (U.S.)   **88**

1959 Royal Enfield Indian (Great Britain)   **90**

1959 Triumph 3TA (Great Britain)   **92**

1961 Matchless G-12 (Great Britain)   **94**

1961 Velocette Venom (Great Britain)   **96**

1962 BSA A65 Star (Great Britain)   **98**

1962 Norton Manx (Great Britain)   **100**

1964 Harley-Davidson FLH (U.S.)   **102**

1964 Triumph Tiger Cub (Great Britain)   **104**

1965 BMW R-27 (Germany)   **106**

1965 DKW Hummel 155 (Germany)   **108**

1965 Ducati 160 Monza Junior (Italy)   **110**

1965 Triumph Bonneville (Great Britain)   **112**

1966 Benelli Fireball Racer (Italy)   **114**

1966 BSA Spitfire (Great Britain)   **116**

1966 Harley-Davidson FLHFB (U.S.)   **118**

1966 Motobi Imperiale Sport (Italy)   **120**

1967 Harley-Davidson XLH (U.S.)   **122**

UNITED STATES GERMANY ITALY JAPAN  GREAT BRITAIN

UNITED STATES

GERMANY

ITALY

JAPAN

GREAT BRITAIN

FOREWORD

Today's wide variety of sophisticated motorcycles can all trace their roots back to 1885, when Gottlieb Daimler and Paul Maybach of Germany constructed a crude, wooden-framed machine powered by a primitive engine and supported by a pair of training wheels. Soon afterward, hundreds of small manufacturers around the world began producing "motorcycles," most employing proprietary engines bolted to simple bicycle frames.

Competition weeded out most of the backyard enterprises early on, but the companies that survived worked feverishly to improve their products. Motorcycles became faster, more reliable, and more purpose-built, weaning themselves from their bicycle heritage. Engines gained more sophisticated intake and ignition systems, various forms of suspension were devised, drum brakes succeeded coaster brakes, transmissions and clutches were added, and kick levers replaced pedals for starting.

Though the state of technology continued to advance over the years, motorcycles of the 1930s were surprisingly modern. It wasn't until the Japanese started a horsepower race in the 1970s that larger strides were made, the resulting Superbikes boasting more power and better brakes.

About that time, the market began to diversify. Scramblers, which were basically street bikes mildly modified for off-pavement use, evolved into more specialized Enduro and Motocross machines. Cruisers offered custom styling right off the showroom floor. Long-distance riders found comfort in the new Touring models, and high-performance Sportbikes that mimicked fully faired racing machines became all the rage.

Virtually every industrialized nation throughout the world hosted at least one motorcycle manufacturer at one time or another, but only five countries produced machines that achieved international popularity: Germany, Great Britain, Japan, Italy, and the United States. All are represented here, and an effort has been made to include examples of the various styles of road-going motorcycles that eventually evolved, from low-slung Cruisers to high-strung Sportbikes—with an early Motocrosser thrown in for good measure.

Motorcycle races have been around almost as long as motorcycles themselves, one of the oldest and most famous being the Isle of Man Tourist Trophy race, held off the coast of England since 1907. Because racing does indeed improve the breed—and hence has played a major role in the technological development of the motorcycle—we have included a few competition machines that gained international fame during the sport's early history. Motorcycles also played an important role in wartime, and for that reason, you will find examples that served their country on the battlefields during World War II.

So that the evolution of the motorcycle can be easily observed, entries are arranged chronologically, starting with the crude conveyances of the early 1900s and running through today's exotic machines. While the Contents list reflects this progression, the Index carries the individual models covered under a given manufacturer's name.

Riders today enjoy machines that are far quicker, safer, more comfortable, and more reliable than their forbearers, yet they still embody the spirit of freedom and adventure exhibited by those hearty soles who made early motorcycles their transportation of choice. *Motorcycle Classics* celebrates some of the most memorable machines of the twentieth century, and salutes the riders—past and present—who have made this sport what it is today.

1904
INDIAN

Indian motorcycles were first built in 1901 by George Hendee and Oscar Hedstrom. The two first met in 1900 at a bicycle racing event. Both had an interest in building a motorized cycle, and they soon joined forces to realize their dream.

This 1904 "humpback" was little different from the 1901 model. The single-cylinder engine was based on an existing DeDion design and generated just over two horsepower. The Aurora Automated Machinery Company was selected to supply the engine castings, and would go on to build the Thor motorcycle using the same castings.

The Indian operated on total-loss systems for both the oil and battery. The engine was an integral part of the diamond frame, which was used until the advent of the loop frame in 1909. Until 1905, the only suspension provided took the form of coils mounted under the saddle. Braking was accomplished by backpedaling, which activated the rear-mounted coaster brake.

Indian claimed to have the first twist-grip spark control in 1904, although the 1904 Curtiss carried a similar device on its handlebars. The first three years of production found all Indians finished in dark blue; in 1904, black and vermillion were added as optional colors. The vermillion would later be known as Indian Red.

YEAR:
1904

MANUFACTURER:
Indian

MODEL:
—

ENGINE TYPE:
Vertical single

DISPLACEMENT:
13 cubic inches

VALVE TRAIN:
Atmospheric intake, side exhaust

CARBURETION:
NA

TRANSMISSION:
Single-speed

FRONT SUSPENSION:
Rigid

FRONT BRAKE(S):
None

REAR SUSPENSION:
Rigid

REAR BRAKE:
Coaster

WEIGHT:
110 pounds

FINAL DRIVE:
Chain

OWNER:
Pete Bollenbach

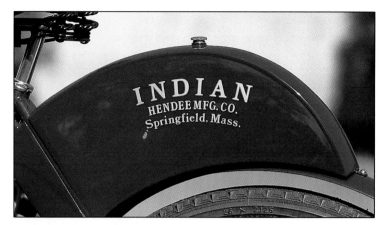

Top left: Like most bicycles—then and today—Indian placed its nameplate on the frame neck. Note intricate jointed shafts that were used before the advent of cables. *Top center:* Single-cylinder engine was spliced into the frame, becoming a structural member. Simple carburetor fed fuel through an atmospheric intake valve. *Top right:* It probably made perfect sense to place the "humpback" fuel tank above the rear fender, but it looks odd in today's light.

1904
MARSH

When motorcycling was in its infancy, the eastern coast of the U.S. found itself crowded with manufacturers of the new machines. Considered to be one of the industry's pioneers, Marsh began assembling its own line of motorcycles in Brockton, Massachusetts, in 1901.

Unlike many early manufacturers, who used engines built by an outside company, Marsh designed and constructed its own powerplants. Both single- and twin-cylinder engines were found in the early offerings from the Marsh factory.

The Marsh single shown here was propelled by a scant three horsepower and sold for $125. The wooden handlebar grips were typically wrapped with cloth tape to help make riding more comfortable. Tools and the battery are stored in a box behind the seat.

As sales increased, Marsh acquired the Metz Company. Metz built both motorcycles and automobiles, and was the first American company to export motorcycles to Europe. After the purchase of Metz, Marsh motorcycles were sold under the M.M. banner until the early Teens, after which time the company ceased production.

YEAR:
1904

MANUFACTURER:
Marsh

MODEL:
—

ENGINE TYPE:
Vertical single

DISPLACEMENT:
27 cubic inches

VALVE TRAIN:
Atmospheric intake,
side exhaust

CARBURETION:
Marsh

TRANSMISSION:
Single-speed

FRONT SUSPENSION:
Rigid

FRONT BRAKE(S):
None

REAR SUSPENSION:
Rigid

REAR BRAKE:
Coaster

WEIGHT:
150 pounds

FINAL DRIVE:
Belt

OWNER:
Tom Baer

As was typical for motorcycles of the period, neither the front nor rear was endowed with any type of suspension system, but at least the hard leather saddle was spring-mounted. The rear coaster brake provided only marginal stopping power. *Left:* Box beneath seat carries the battery for the constant-loss electrical system; there is no generator. Chrome lever on side of fuel tank is the compression release, which cracks the exhaust valve open to make starting easier.

1910
EMBLEM

The Emblem Manufacturing Company was one of the nearly 300 motorcycle producers in the United States in the early 1900s. Claiming "Class, Power, Speed & Satisfaction," Emblem had high hopes of achieving success in a crowded market.

The buyer of an Emblem in 1910 had several configurations from which to choose. The entry-level model was driven by a four-horsepower, single-cylinder engine that was fitted with V-belt drive and sold for $200. For $260, the top-of-the-line model came equipped with a seven-horsepower twin-cylinder engine that drove a flat belt with an adjustable idler wheel.

All Emblems were fitted with three batteries and a coil, but a Herz magneto could be added for an additional $25. For another $15, the owner could add the "Free Engine Pulley" option, which was an early attempt at a clutch mechanism.

Emblems were sold in the U.S. between 1909 and 1918, but like many other makes, fell victim to the wartime economy of World War I. However, a 531-cc model was exported to Europe as late as 1925.

YEAR:
1910

MANUFACTURER:
Emblem

MODEL:
—

ENGINE TYPE:
Vertical single

DISPLACEMENT:
38 cubic inches

VALVE TRAIN:
Atmospheric intake, side exhaust

CARBURETION:
Emblem

TRANSMISSION:
Single-speed

FRONT SUSPENSION:
Leading link with coil spring

FRONT BRAKE(S):
None

REAR SUSPENSION:
Rigid

REAR BRAKE:
Coaster

WEIGHT
NA

FINAL DRIVE:
Belt

OWNER:
Pete Bollenbach

Below: Tall lever on left side of tank controlled the "Free Engine Pulley," an early form of clutch.
Left: Engine used an atmospheric intake valve, which was opened by cylinder suction rather than mechanical means. It is situated below the gold-colored barrel on top of the cylinder. Diagonal rod going to base of exhaust-valve spring is for the compression release, which would hold the valve open slightly to ease starting.

1911
EXCELSIOR SINGLE

Since the inception of the Excelsior Supply & Manufacturing Company in 1907, its motorcycles were in a constant state of improvement. Still a part of the larger Schwinn Bicycle concern, there was plenty of research and development talent on tap.

For 1911, Excelsior offered both single- and twin-cylinder models. Either could be ordered with a magneto or battery electrical system. Both were belt driven, as chain drive would not arrive until 1913.

The 1912 Excelsiors would remain almost identical to the 1911 models, except for price. As an additional incentive to buy an Excelsior, the cost of the entire line was lowered. A savings of $25 was touted on the 1912 single over the same machine in 1911.

Before production ceased in 1931, Excelsior was considered to be one of the "Big Three" American motorcycle companies, the others being Harley-Davidson and Indian. These three were the only motorcycles contracted for use by the U.S. Army in the First World War.

YEAR:
1911

MANUFACTURER:
Excelsior

MODEL:
Single

ENGINE TYPE:
Vertical single

DISPLACEMENT:
499 cc (approx. 30 cubic inches)

VALVE TRAIN:
Overhead intake, side exhaust

CARBURETION:
NA

TRANSMISSION:
Single-speed

FRONT SUSPENSION:
Leading link with coil springs

FRONT BRAKE(S):
None

REAR SUSPENSION:
Rigid

REAR BRAKE:
Coaster

WEIGHT:
NA

FINAL DRIVE:
Belt

OWNER:
R. B. McClean

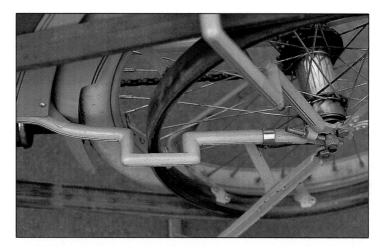

Left: Before the advent of modern cables, control motions were transferred by intricate jointed shafts. *Below:* The Excelsior's rear frame tubes had to be altered to clear the large drive pulley.

1911
MINNEAPOLIS DELIVERY

Between 1903 and the start of World War I, motorcycle "manufacturers" were springing up like weeds all around the country. Oftentimes, these machines were named after the city in which they were built. One such example is the Minneapolis.

Although the company's history is a bit sketchy, early Minneapolis models carried engines produced by Thor, itself a builder of motorcycles. But starting in 1910, Minneapolis began using its own engines.

Dubbed the "Big 5," this single-cylinder engine produced five horsepower, hence the name. Bucking the contemporary trend of using an overhead intake valve and side exhaust valve (known as an F-head or IOE, Intake Over Exhaust), Minneapolis stuck with the old side-valve arrangement (otherwise known as a flathead, with both valves in the block to the side of the piston).

Minneapolis offered a choice of a single- or two-speed gearbox, though if the former was chosen initially, the second ratio could be added at a later time. On the three-wheel version, the use of a crank for starting was also passé, as most others had gone to kick starters.

This maroon three-wheeler is probably the only one of its kind ever produced by Minneapolis. According to the sales literature, all other motorcycles the company built (just five or six in total) were finished in green.

As with so many other manufacturers, Minneapolis led a brief life. The war played a critical role in the making and breaking of motorcycle companies, and unfortunately, Minneapolis was not one of the survivors.

YEAR:
1911

MANUFACTURER:
Minneapolis

MODEL:
Delivery

ENGINE TYPE:
Vertical single

DISPLACEMENT:
36 cubic inches

VALVE TRAIN:
Side valves

CARBURETION:
Schebler

TRANSMISSION:
One or two speeds

FRONT SUSPENSION:
Live axle with leaf springs

FRONT BRAKE(S):
None

REAR SUSPENSION:
Rigid

REAR BRAKE:
Drum

WEIGHT:
NA

FINAL DRIVE:
Chain

OWNER:
Charles Petty

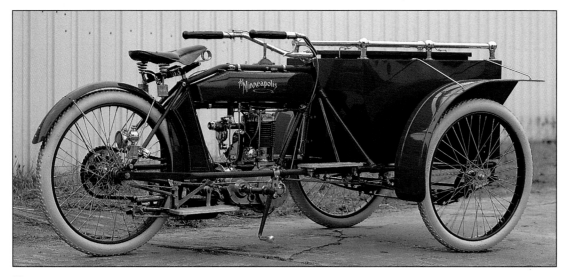

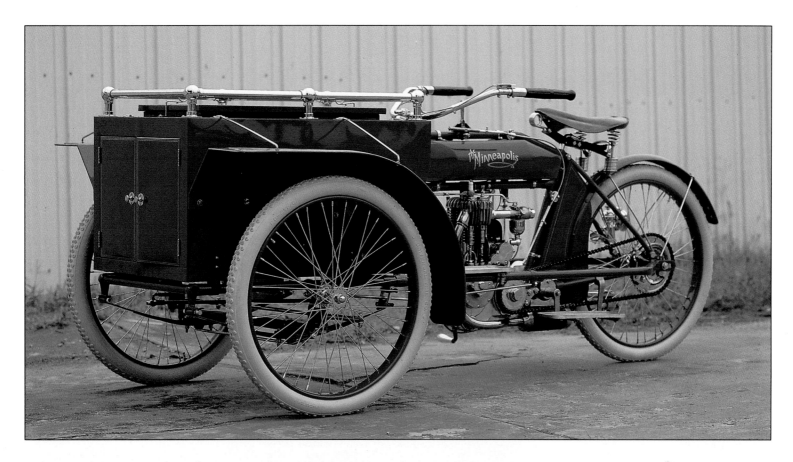

This one-of-a-kind Minneapolis demonstrates how early motorcycles were used for more than just simple transportation. *Opposite page:* Red handle below engine is a hand-operated crank starter. *Above:* Handlebars control an automotive-type steering linkage to turn the front wheels. *Left:* Magneto, directly behind cylinder, can be adjusted to control spark timing.

1912
HARLEY-DAVIDSON X8A

Harley-Davidson's first motorcycle, little more than a bicycle with a single-cylinder three-horsepower engine mounted within the frame tubes, was built in 1903. Though the V-twins that would make the company famous appeared six years later, single-cylinder machines continued to represent the bulk of Harley's sales. By 1912, public demand for more power was answered with the X8A, which was powered by a 30-cubic-inch single that produced 4.3 horsepower.

A hand-operated oil pump was added to augment the existing gravity-feed system, and a magneto ignition was used to facilitate easier starting. Also debuting this year was the "Free Wheel Control," one of the industry's first clutch systems. With it, smooth takeoffs from a standing start were possible for the first time.

The issue of comfort was also addressed. Mounted inside the vertical frame tube was a coil spring used to cushion the seat post, while the rear of the seat was supported by two more coils. Dubbed the "Full Floeting" saddle, it was hardly a substitute for a real rear suspension, but it was the best Harley riders would get for another 45 years.

YEAR:
1912

MANUFACTURER:
Harley-Davidson

MODEL:
X8A

ENGINE TYPE:
Vertical single

DISPLACEMENT:
30 cubic inches

VALVE TRAIN:
Atmospheric intake,
side exhaust

CARBURETION:
Schebler

TRANSMISSION:
Single-speed

FRONT SUSPENSION:
Leading link with coil springs

FRONT BRAKE(S):
None

REAR SUSPENSION:
Rigid

REAR BRAKE:
Coaster

WEIGHT:
260 pounds

FINAL DRIVE:
Belt

OWNER:
Henry Hardin Family

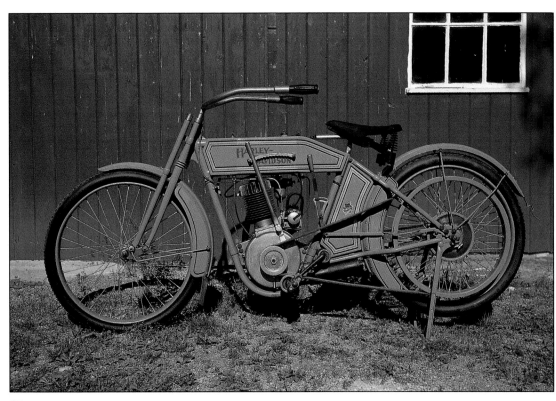

Opposite page: Tall lever on left side of tank activated the "Free Wheel Control," Harley's early clutch system. *Above:* While many companies had gone to a mechanical intake valve by this time, the X8A stuck with an atmospheric intake valve, located beneath the small dome at the top of the engine. *Left:* Clip on rear fender held the rear support stand up while the bike was moving.

1913
EXCELSIOR 7-C

Mr. Ignatz Schwinn had been in the business of building bicycles for several years when he decided to capitalize on the motorcycling craze that was sweeping the nation. By combining a 500-cc Dion single-cylinder engine with a stout bicycle frame, Schwinn gave birth to the first Excelsior motorcycle in 1907—or at least the first Excelsior motorcycle to be built in the United States. Strangely, the name was already in use on motorcycles produced by separate companies in both Germany and England.

The Excelsior underwent continuous improvements, and in 1910 was joined by an 800-cc V-twin. The V-twin soon grew to 1000 ccs, gaining chain drive to replace the former belt, which was the state of engineering when this 1913 model was built.

Since his interest in the world of motorcycles was growing, Ignatz Schwinn purchased the financially troubled Henderson Company in 1917 and expanded his line to include Henderson's inline-four model. This new acquisition pushed the Excelsiors into the shadows as the big Henderson grew in popularity.

But just as quickly as the inspiration had come, Ignatz Schwinn seemed to lose interest in motorcycling. By 1931, both the Henderson and the Excelsior had joined the growing number of marques that had blossomed during motorcycling's boom years, only to succumb to stiff competition and a depressed economy in the early '30s.

YEAR:
1913

MANUFACTURER:
Excelsior

MODEL:
7-C

ENGINE TYPE:
V-twin

DISPLACEMENT:
1000 cc (approx. 61 cubic inches)

VALVE TRAIN:
Overhead intake, side exhaust

CARBURETION:
Schebler

TRANSMISSION:
Single-speed

FRONT SUSPENSION:
Trailing link with leaf spring

FRONT BRAKE(S):
None

REAR SUSPENSION:
Rigid

REAR BRAKE:
Coaster

WEIGHT:
Approx. 275 pounds

FINAL DRIVE:
Chain

OWNER:
Henry Hardin Family

During its heyday, Chicago-based Excelsior was a big name in motorcycling, often running third in sales behind Harley-Davidson and Indian. Though this 1913 Excelsior has a single-speed transmission, subsequent models drove through a three-speed unit. Big V-twin used overhead intake valves that were actuated by exposed pushrods and rocker arms. Lacking any kind of replenished lubrication, these parts undoubtedly required frequent replacement—but at least they were easy to get to. Note dimple in tank (above) that was needed to clear the valve-train components.

1913
INDIAN SINGLE

Though Indian began with single-cylinder machines in 1904, the company was better known for its V-twins, which debuted in 1907. They sold side-by-side for some time, but V-twins were usually more popular and it's not difficult to see why: in 1913, for example, a four-horsepower single cost $200; a seven-horsepower twin went for $250. Customer preference for power was obvious, as singles accounted for only ten percent of production that year.

Also by that time, Indian could boast of 1,500 dealerships throughout the U.S. and overseas, and a full quarter of all Indians built were exported to other countries. Quality control was an important ingredient in the company's success, and every 100th bike to roll off the assembly line was given a thorough road test prior to delivery.

Indian's first swingarm rear suspension appeared in 1913, termed the "Cradle Spring Frame." Though a rigid frame was still available, our featured Single carries the sprung rear end, with the swingarm actuating vertical rods that pressed against leaf springs anchored to the frame beneath the seat. The trailing-link front suspension was of a similar design. Note that the lone cylinder is mounted in a "reclined" position; most singles had the cylinder leaning forward, parallel with the front frame tube.

Footboards and a luggage rack were now standard equipment, and Indian Red was the only color choice due to the elimination of Dark Indian Blue as an option.

YEAR:
1913

MANUFACTURER:
Indian

MODEL:
Single

ENGINE TYPE:
Vertical single

DISPLACEMENT:
30 cubic inches

VALVE TRAIN:
Overhead intake, side exhaust

CARBURETION:
Schriver

TRANSMISSION:
Single-speed

FRONT SUSPENSION:
Trailing link with leaf spring

FRONT BRAKE(S):
None

REAR SUSPENSION:
Swingarm with leaf springs

REAR BRAKE:
Coaster

WEIGHT:
NA

FINAL DRIVE:
Chain

OWNER:
Elden Raasch

Far left: Tall lever on left side of tank actuated the clutch. *Left:* Small hand pump attached to the oil tank allowed the rider to feed more oil to the engine during periods of hard use or when going uphill. *Below:* Leaf-spring front suspension was used on larger Indians through the 1930s.

1913
READING STANDARD

Reading Standard began selling 499-cc single-cylinder motorcycles in 1903. Later models were powered by V-twin engines of 990 and 1170 ccs.

Advertised as "R-S" motorcycles, Reading Standards were sold across the country. The company began entering competitive events in 1907, and won its first 1000-mile endurance race the same year.

By 1910, however, Reading Standard had tired of racing, and decided to focus its attention on selling more units at the retail level. The decision was perhaps a bit late; by 1914, business had already begun to look grim.

A last-ditch effort saw Reading Standard offering a 61-cubic-inch overhead-valve model built from a Cyclone, with changes made to the frame, tank, and front forks. But in 1922, Reading Standard sold out to the Cleveland Motorcycle company, which offered a Reading Standard model in 1923 as a low-dollar alternative to its existing motorcycles. The following year, Cleveland put its own line of machinery up for sale, and the Reading Standard name slipped into oblivion.

YEAR:
1913

MANUFACTURER:
Reading Standard

MODEL:
—

ENGINE TYPE:
V-twin

DISPLACEMENT:
990 cc (approx. 61 cubic inches)

VALVE TRAIN:
Side valves

CARBURETION:
Schebler

TRANSMISSION:
Single-speed

FRONT SUSPENSION:
Leading link with enclosed coil spring

FRONT BRAKE(S):
None

REAR SUSPENSION:
Rigid

REAR BRAKE:
Coaster

WEIGHT:
325 pounds

FINAL DRIVE:
Chain

OWNER:
R. B. McClean

Bottom left: Cylindrical canister mounted to the handlebars carried acetylene fuel for the Prest-O-Lite headlamp. *Bottom right:* Like most bikes of the era, the Reading Standard's engine utilized a "total loss" lubrication system; oil stored in the overhead tank would flow down through the engine and drip out onto the ground. Some oil was carried in the sump, however, and when it was initially filled after an oil change, oil would be added until it reached the proper level in this sight glass.

27

1913
SCHICKEL BIG 5

In 1912, a new player entered the already-crowded motorcycle marketplace. Hailing from Stamford, Connecticut, the Schickel burst onto the scene powered by a single-cylinder two-stroke engine. As rare as two-strokes were at the time, Schickel was hardly the first manufacturer to use them; several years earlier, the British-built Scott was introduced with a single-cylinder two-stroke that was water-cooled.

The 648-cc engine in the Schickel was cradled within a frame made of lightweight cast alloy. In keeping with the times, the trailing-link front fork was suspended with small coil springs that provided rather limited travel—and relatively little comfort. The seat was cushioned by its own set of springs, which likewise did little good.

When compared to the buckboard ride that punished the driver, passengers in the Dunham sidecar rode in the lap of luxury. Hung from large leaf springs and trimmed with a padded perch, the sidecar was a pleasant venue from which to survey the countryside.

Schickels unfortunately led a short life. Due to the flood of machines on the market and the resulting competition, the company ceased production in 1915.

YEAR:
1913

MANUFACTURER:
Schickel

MODEL:
Big 5

ENGINE TYPE:
Vertical single

DISPLACEMENT:
648 cc (approx. 45 cubic inches)

VALVE TRAIN:
Two-stroke

CARBURETION:
NA

TRANSMISSION:
Single-speed

FRONT SUSPENSION:
Trailing link with coil springs

FRONT BRAKE(S):
None

REAR SUSPENSION:
Rigid

REAR BRAKE:
Coaster

WEIGHT:
NA

FINAL DRIVE:
Belt

OWNER:
R. B. McClean

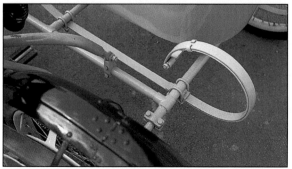

Far left: Metal tank on handlebars fed fuel to the acetylene headlight. *Left:* Dunham sidecar was supported by an elliptical leaf spring that provided a modicum of comfort to the rider. In order to ease travel in deeply rutted roadways, the outer wheel of the sidecar could be adjusted to fit the width of the ruts in the road.

1914
SEARS DELUXE

In the early catalogs from Sears and Roebuck, you could order almost anything—including a house. But it was in the 1912 catalog that Sears offered its first motorcycle.

This 1914 magneto model, complete with the Deluxe "Big Five" engine, sold for $197.50 and was claimed to have nearly the same power as the larger twin-cylinder models. These single-cylinder versions were available with either batteries or a Bosch magneto. Two twin-cylinder motorcycles were offered, one producing seven horsepower, the other producing nine. The engines in all Sears machines were manufactured by Spake, which sold engines to a variety of builders.

As with most makers of motorcycles in this period, Sears claimed high quality and proven performance for its models. The handlebars were made of double-reinforced tubing and the fuel tank was formed out of anti-rust material. A trailing-link fork with leaf spring handled suspension chores in front, but a seat mounted on coil springs had to make do in the rear.

Sears only sold these early motorcycles until 1916, when they were removed from the catalog. But between 1953 and 1963, Sears offered a line of cycles manufactured by Puch under the Sears-Allstate moniker.

YEAR:
1914

MANUFACTURER:
Sears

MODEL:
Deluxe

ENGINE TYPE:
Vertical single

DISPLACEMENT:
35 cubic inches

VALVE TRAIN:
Overhead intake, side exhaust

CARBURETION:
NA

TRANSMISSION:
Two-speed rear hub

FRONT SUSPENSION:
Trailing link with leaf spring

FRONT BRAKE(S):
None

REAR SUSPENSION:
Rigid

REAR BRAKE:
External band

WEIGHT:
200 pounds

FINAL DRIVE:
Chain

OWNER:
Pete Bollenbach

Opposite page: Like Indian, Sears used leaf-spring front suspension. Lever at side of tank controls the clutch; pedal at lever's base activates the two-speed rear hub. *Top and above:* Spiral gear on rear hub drives the speedometer, mounted on top of the gas tank. Sears used parts supplied by several companies, including a magneto made by German-based Bosch.

1915
CYCLONE RACER

Though Cyclones enjoyed a production run of only four years, their impact on motorcycle racing far exceeded their meager numbers. Built by the Joerns Manufacturing Company from 1911 to 1915, they recorded an impressive string of victories on the dirt and board tracks around the country.

Most of this success can be attributed to the Cyclone's 61-cubic-inch engine. While the V-twin layout was not uncommon, the mechanical details were. Valves were actuated by a single overhead camshaft driven by bevel gears; this was at a time when most engines were flatheads, or at best had overhead intakes and side exhausts. With a Bosch magneto supplying the spark, the mighty V-twin redlined at an impressive 5000 rpm, making the Cyclone moniker very appropriate indeed.

As was common on racing bikes of the era, the Cyclone had no transmission or clutch; it made do with direct chain drive and pedals to get it moving. It also had no suspension system (aside from high-pressure air in the tires) and no brakes. Slowing down was accomplished by hitting the kill switch—or a stationary object.

Capable of running at speeds in excess of 110 mph, Cyclones dominated the competition circuit until Harley-Davidson and Indian began campaigning special eight-valve racing engines. At that point, Joerns Manufacturing Company pulled the plug on the Cyclone, concentrating instead on more civilized motorcycles.

YEAR:
1915

MANUFACTURER:
Joerns Manufacturing Company

MODEL:
Cyclone racer

ENGINE TYPE:
V-twin

DISPLACEMENT:
61 cubic inches

VALVE TRAIN:
Single overhead cam

CARBURETION:
NA

TRANSMISSION:
Direct drive

FRONT SUSPENSION:
Rigid

FRONT BRAKE(S):
None

REAR SUSPENSION:
Rigid

REAR BRAKE:
None

WEIGHT:
250 pounds

FINAL DRIVE:
Chain

OWNER:
E. J. Cole

Top: As on current bikes, right handgrip controlled the throttle. Note abbreviated exhaust pipes. *Above:* Hand pump on oil tank allowed rider to feed additional oil to the engine. Small knob above left hand grip is the kill switch for the ignition—the only form of "braking" the rider had. Drive chain had been removed so that the bike could be rolled without turning over the engine, as there is no clutch. *Right:* Overhead cam actuated valves through forked rocker arms, which ran *au natural.*

1915
EMBLEM TWIN

By 1915, motorcycle manufacturers were springing up like weeds and a horsepower race was in progress. Each manufacturer claimed to outrun, outclimb, or outlast all the rest, and Emblem was no exception.

Emblem advertising that year stated that their twin displaced 76.6 cubic inches, "16 more than any other motorcycle motor." The intake valve was now mechanically actuated, an improvement over the more common suction type. According to the Emblem sales brochures, each Emblem Twin had to be ridden in excess of 70 miles per hour before it would be shipped. A test card accompanied each bike that indicated the speed that had been reached.

Technical enhancements for the 1915 Emblem made riding a simpler, more enjoyable task. The step starter took less effort than the typical kick-start mechanism, and the two speeds were selected with a foot control. A high-tension magneto provided more than enough energy to keep the twin cylinders firing.

YEAR:
1915

MANUFACTURER:
Emblem

MODEL:
Twin

ENGINE TYPE:
V-twin

DISPLACEMENT:
76 cubic inches

VALVE TRAIN:
Overhead intake, side exhaust

CARBURETION:
NA

TRANSMISSION:
Two-speed, foot shift

FRONT SUSPENSION:
Leading link with coil spring

FRONT BRAKE(S):
None

REAR SUSPENSION:
Rigid

REAR BRAKE:
Coaster

WEIGHT:
NA

FINAL DRIVE:
Chain

OWNER:
E. J. Cole

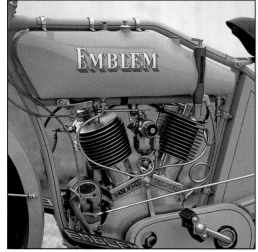

Left: Like many engines of the era, the overhead intake valves were actuated through exposed push rods and rocker arms. The exhaust valve springs and pushrods can be seen flanking the exhaust pipes. *Far left:* A Herz magneto supplied spark to the big V-twin. Copper-colored cylinder on the side of the tank is a hand pump that was used to feed additional oil to the engine when it was under stress.

1920
HARLEY-DAVIDSON L20T

After the 1909 introduction of the V-twin that would make the company famous, Harley-Davidson's sales—and fortunes—began climbing. By 1920, manufacturing facilities had been expanded to keep up with the increased demand, allowing for production of up to 35,000 motorcycles per year.

While little changed in appearance from its predecessors, the 1920 edition of the 61-cubic-inch V-twin sported new cylinders and protective caps over the previously exposed springs at the base of the pushrods. Also new was a dust cover for the clutch.

Though still fired by a magneto ignition, L20Ts built late in the model year adopted a generator for the first time. The engine also featured screw-out primer cups that would allow the rider to squirt a small amount of fuel directly into the cylinder to facilitate cold-weather starting.

Despite these improvements, Harley-Davidson was not able to sell enough motorcycles to keep the expanded factory running at capacity—nor would it until after World War II. Yet sales of this 1920 L20T reached a respectable 28,000 units, enough to keep the company prosperous at a time when many manufacturers were going belly-up.

YEAR:
1920

MANUFACTURER:
Harley-Davidson

MODEL:
L20T

ENGINE TYPE:
V-twin

DISPLACEMENT:
61 cubic inches

VALVE TRAIN:
Overhead intake, side exhaust

CARBURETION:
Schebler

TRANSMISSION:
Three-speed, hand shift

FRONT SUSPENSION:
Leading link with coil springs

FRONT BRAKE(S):
None

REAR SUSPENSION:
Rigid

REAR BRAKE:
External band

WEIGHT:
325 pounds

FINAL DRIVE:
Chain

OWNER:
Henry Hardin family

By the early 1920s, Harley-Davidson used kick starters in place of pedals, as did many other manufacturers, and motorcycles took a giant step forward from their bicycle heritage. They also gained three-speed transmissions; the shift lever is beside the tank *(top)*, while the clutch can be activated with either a hand lever, located beneath the seat, or a foot pedal *(above right)*. *Left:* Mechanical overhead intake valves were actuated through exposed rocker arms. *Above center:* Electric horn sits below the headlight.

1927
HARLEY-DAVIDSON BA

The 21-cubic-inch Harley single was built for ten years, but never gained widespread popularity in the U.S. However, the competition version, known as the "peashooter," claimed many victories under the control of Joe Petrali during the same ten-year period.

During its production, the single came in four versions that included both side-valve and overhead-valve models. The BA was given aluminum pistons and the 1927 version featured Ricardo cylinder heads that forced the air/fuel mixture towards the spark for better combustion. It was also equipped with a generator while earlier versions were fitted only with batteries. Rated at 3.3 horsepower, the BA was capable of reaching speeds of nearly 65 mph.

The frames of the '27 BAs were still made from seamless, high-carbon steel tube, but were now reinforced at several points. Mounting tabs were also beefed up for added durability. Another improvement for 1927 was a muffler that reduced back pressure and increased performance.

America's preference for big, powerful twins led to the demise of these single-cylinder models. Harley made several attempts at selling singles in the coming years, but it was always V-twins for which the company was best known.

YEAR:
1927

MANUFACTURER:
Harley-Davidson

MODEL:
BA

ENGINE TYPE:
Vertical single

DISPLACEMENT:
21 cubic inches

VALVE TRAIN:
Side valves

CARBURETION:
Schebler

TRANSMISSION:
Three-speed, hand shift

FRONT SUSPENSION:
Leading link with coil springs

FRONT BRAKE(S):
None

REAR SUSPENSION:
Rigid

REAR BRAKE:
Coaster

WEIGHT:
NA

FINAL DRIVE:
Chain

OWNER:
Tom Baer

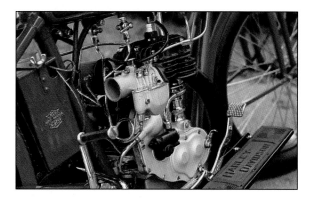

Left: Shift lever moved from low gear (all the way forward) to neutral, second, and then third (all the way back) through a staggered gate. *Above and far left:* Sprouting numerous knobs, levers, and cables, the simple carburetor looks rather complex.

1930
HARLEY-DAVIDSON MODEL V

In 1930, a vast majority of the U.S. population was still reeling from the Great Depression. There were, however, a few well-heeled individuals left with the desire to own a Harley-Davidson.

There were only six models available in 1930, down from thirteen the previous year; even the great Harley-Davidson was feeling the effect of the financial troubles in the U.S. The Model V carried a revised 74-cubic-inch engine and was offered in two versions: the VL, with high-compression heads; and the VS, with lower-compression heads and gearing that made it more suitable for use with a sidecar or as a package van.

Model Vs came equipped with twin headlights and a cylindrical steel tool can on the front fork, but the tool can and second headlight were often removed for a sleeker look and less noise. The Vs sold for $340, which was akin to a king's ransom during the Depression.

Nevertheless, Harley's sales in 1930 totaled over 17,000 units—but would drop to less than 4000 in 1933 when the economy finally hit bottom.

YEAR:
1930

MANUFACTURER:
Harley-Davidson

MODEL:
Model V

ENGINE TYPE:
V-twin

DISPLACEMENT:
74 cubic inches

VALVE TRAIN:
Side valves

CARBURETION:
Schebler

TRANSMISSION:
Three-speed, hand shift

FRONT SUSPENSION:
Leading link with coil springs

FRONT BRAKE(S):
Drum

REAR SUSPENSION:
Rigid

REAR BRAKE:
Drum

WEIGHT:
NA

FINAL DRIVE:
Chain

OWNER:
Illinois Harley-Davidson

Opposite page: Speedometer, mounted atop the fuel tank, was driven off a large ring gear attached to the rear wheel. *Above:* Since the Model V itself offered no accommodations for a passenger, sidecars were popular for transporting a traveling companion. Suspended on leaf springs and fitted with a windshield, padded seat, and enclosed body, the sidecar offered the passenger a much more hospitable environment than the rider enjoyed.

1936
DKW SB 500 A

DKW began building motorcycles in 1919, starting with a one-horsepower engine on a bicycle frame. By the 1930s, the company had grown to be the world's largest producer of motorcycles. Not only did DKW build its own machines, it also supplied two-stroke engines to other manufacturers. In addition, the company built automobiles from 1929 until the late Sixties.

Before the outbreak of World War II, DKW had amassed an impressive racing record, including a win at the Isle of Man TT event in 1938. During the war, DKWs saw extensive use on battlefields throughout Europe.

The 494-cc engine in the SB 500 A resulted from combining two separate 247-cc cylinders on a single block. Fed by a Bing carburetor, the two-stroke engine produced 15 horsepower. As did many American bikes of the period, the DKW had a three-speed transmission with a hand shifter and foot-operated clutch.

"A" models differed from regular SB 500s in that they had a stronger frame fitted with a larger fuel tank and twin headlights. They also had electric start, a rare feature for that time; by contrast, Harley-Davidson didn't offer an electric starter until 1965.

YEAR:
1936

MANUFACTURER:
DKW

MODEL:
SB 500 A

ENGINE TYPE:
Vertical twin

DISPLACEMENT:
494 cc (approx. 30 cubic inches)

VALVE TRAIN:
Two-stroke

CARBURETION:
Bing

TRANSMISSION:
Three-speed, hand shift

FRONT SUSPENSION:
Girder fork with coil spring

FRONT BRAKE(S):
Drum

REAR SUSPENSION:
Rigid

REAR BRAKE:
Drum

WEIGHT:
NA

FINAL DRIVE:
Chain

OWNER:
Jim Kersting Family Collection

Distinctive twin headlights really made this DKW stand out—particularly at night. Another unusual feature was electric starting, which was augmented by a left-side kick starter. DKW joined Germany's Auto Union group early on, as symbolized by the four overlapping circles on the tank's knee pad—a trademark still used on Audi automobiles. DKW's popularity waned during the 1950s, and what was once the world's largest producer of motorcycles closed its doors in the mid-Sixties.

1937
HARLEY-DAVIDSON ULH

Even as the new-for-1936 overhead-valve "Knucklehead" was selling at a record pace, Harley-Davidson continued to improve its side-valve models. For 1937, an 80-cubic-inch version was released and the ULH model was recommended for use with a sidecar.

Internal engine changes were abundant. A larger flywheel was installed to smooth out the power flow and the latest combustion chamber provided additional energy with every firing of the spark plugs. On the outside of the engine the cylinder was cast with deeper fins to assist in the dissipation of heat. The Y-type intake manifold from the 45- and 74-cubic-inch models was now incorporated into the big twin. A dry-sump oiling system was employed to ensure proper lubrication.

This 1937 ULH was the only prewar model to feature an oil tank painted the same color as the fuel tank and fenders. A stronger double-loop frame was now in place to strengthen the ULH's platform. A tubular front fork was borrowed from the smaller side-valve models, though in this application it carried a leading link actuating coil springs to make the ride more comfortable. The black instrument panel continued to include the speedometer, ammeter, and oil pressure gauge, and would not be altered until the 1938 models arrived.

YEAR:
1937

MANUFACTURER:
Harley-Davidson

MODEL:
ULH

ENGINE TYPE:
V-twin

DISPLACEMENT:
80 cubic inches

VALVE TRAIN:
Side valves

CARBURETION:
NA

TRANSMISSION:
Four-speed, hand shift

FRONT SUSPENSION:
Leading link with coil springs

FRONT BRAKE(S):
Drum

REAR SUSPENSION:
Rigid

REAR BRAKE:
Drum

WEIGHT
NA

FINAL DRIVE:
Chain

OWNER:
"Wheels Through Time"
museum

Top: Driving lights that flanked the original headlight were popular accessories of the day, and greatly increased nighttime visibility. *Left:* Instrument panel included ammeter and oil pressure gauges; later models would substitute warning lights for the gauges. *Above:* "Fishtail" mufflers were used by Harley throughout the Thirties.

1937
INDIAN CHIEF

In the middle of the 1930s, the battle between Indian and Harley-Davidson was heating up. Both on and off the track, an intense case of one-upmanship was taking place. There was a minor intrusion from overseas, but the new British machines were not yet equipped to compete.

As in previous years, the Chief was Indian's premium offering, and it saw several changes for 1937. Due to popular demand, the shift lever was moved to the front of the gas tank—resulting in a rather balky shift linkage. Another unfavorable revision was the external oil lines, which tended to mist the outside of the engine with oil. However, some changes made to the Chief were for the better, such as a larger chain guard to protect the four-row drive chain.

Due to Indian's ownership by DuPont, an endless variety of colors were made available to the buyer of a Chief. For only $5, any combination of DuPont paints could be chosen for application.

Even though the Chief touted numerous mechanical superiorities, Harley-Davidson was already beginning to dominate the market and would reign supreme after the Second World War.

YEAR:
1937

MANUFACTURER:
Indian

MODEL:
Chief

ENGINE TYPE:
V-twin

DISPLACEMENT:
74 cubic inches

VALVE TRAIN:
Side valves

CARBURETION:
NA

TRANSMISSION:
Three-speed, hand shift
(four-speed optional)

FRONT SUSPENSION:
Trailing link with leaf spring

FRONT BRAKE(S):
Drum

REAR SUSPENSION:
Rigid

REAR BRAKE:
Drum

WEIGHT:
480 pounds

FINAL DRIVE:
Chain

OWNER:
Pete Bollenbach

Opposite page: This Indian is equipped with an optional passenger's seat, which consists of a sprung saddle and elaborate bracing struts that include a hand rail and fold-down foot pegs. Saddle bags and a protective windscreen *(left)* were other popular options. *Above:* The two forward gas caps are for filling the split fuel tank; the right rear cap is for oil.

1938
BMW KOMPRESSOR

As evidenced by its blue and white logo, which is supposed to represent a spinning propeller, BMW started out building aircraft engines. In 1921 the company began building smaller engines that were used by other motorcycle manufacturers, but it wasn't until 1923 that BMW built its own bikes.

Those early 500-cc machines had a horizontally opposed twin-cylinder engine, a configuration the company became famous for and still uses today. In the mid-Thirties, BMW was one of the first manufacturers to use modern telescopic forks.

About that same time, the company began to get involved in racing. Though successful at first, the competition soon became stiff, and BMW's machines were being outgunned on a regular basis. The Kompressor model of 1938 reversed that trend using a 492-cc engine with a supercharger mounted to the front of the crankshaft.

Though the bike pictured is lacking its supercharger, it is otherwise a fine representation of the BMW racing machines that gained dominance in the days before World War II. After the war, superchargers were banned on racing machines in order to create a more level playing field.

YEAR:
1938

MANUFACTURER:
BMW

MODEL:
Kompressor

ENGINE TYPE:
Horizontally opposed twin

DISPLACEMENT:
492 cc (approx. 30 cubic inches)

VALVE TRAIN:
Overhead valves

CARBURETION:
Dell'Orto

TRANSMISSION:
Five-speed, foot shift

FRONT SUSPENSION:
Telescopic

FRONT BRAKE(S):
Drum

REAR SUSPENSION:
Plunger-type with coil springs

REAR BRAKE:
Drum

WEIGHT:
302 pounds

FINAL DRIVE:
Shaft

OWNER:
Erich Bley

Left: As it does today, BMW used shaft drive for its early racers, though the shafts weren't enclosed as was the practice on later models. Plunger-type rear suspension is similar in design to what Indian later adopted for its motorcycles. *Far left:* Our featured bike is missing the supercharger that was originally mounted at the forward end of the engine case. A round silver cover is mounted in its place.

1938
HARLEY-DAVIDSON MODEL U

It had been well over three decades since the first motorcycle made its presence known, and the world was discovering more applications for this versatile machine everyday. Still considered to be the biggest kid on the block, Harley-Davidson found its products being put to use all around the globe.

Sidecars had been a popular ad-on since the First World War to transport a passenger in style and comfort. Many businesses, including the U.S. Post Office, found that motorcycles made exceptional delivery vehicles. By attaching a cargo box to a two-wheeled vehicle, you could easily travel to many spots not accessible with a car or truck.

This 1938 Model U has been outfitted with a Harley-Davidson Model M package van of the same year. The full-size third wheel kept the ride smooth even when traveling over unpaved roads.

The Model U was built around the 74-cubic-inch, medium-compression engine. Though not the most powerful engine available, the 74 had a proven track record of durability.

Motorcycle delivery vehicles faded from the scene with the advent of small, efficient four-wheeled vehicles and the modernization of American roadways.

YEAR:
1938

MANUFACTURER:
Harley-Davidson

MODEL:
U

ENGINE TYPE:
V-twin

DISPLACEMENT:
74 cubic inches

VALVE TRAIN:
Side valves

CARBURETION:
Linkert

TRANSMISSION:
Three-speed, hand shift, with reverse

FRONT SUSPENSION:
Leading link with coil springs

FRONT BRAKE(S):
Drum

REAR SUSPENSION:
Rigid

REAR BRAKE:
Drum

WEIGHT:
NA

FINAL DRIVE:
Chain

OWNER:
Al and Pat Doerman

Bottom left: Like most sidecars, the package van was mounted on leaf springs; it also had a small door spring in front to help stabilize the box. Note that the van's fender and the motorcycle's front fender wear matching running lights. *Above and below:* The chrome shift lever beside the tank positioned first gear all the way forward and third gear all the way back; second sat in the middle of the staggered shift pattern, with neutral between first and second.

1938
HARLEY-DAVIDSON UL

After recovering from a difficult period in the early Thirties, Harley-Davidson was poised to forge ahead with a complete lineup that included 11 different models. They were built around V-twin engines of 61, 74, or 80 cubic inches, all of which shared several components. However, the 61-cubic-inch engine was the famous "Knucklehead" with overhead valves, while the 74- and 80-cubic-inch engines had side valves.

The UL was a Sport Solo model with a 74-cubic-inch "flathead" powerplant. Like other big twins of 1938, it carried numerous—though subtle—changes. Frames were strengthened and higher handlebars resulted in a more comfortable riding position. The instrument panel was simplified by replacing the ammeter with a red warning lamp and the oil-pressure gauge with a green lamp. The speedometer calibration was now marked off in two-mile-per-hour increments instead of the previous five, and new colors and striping were made available.

With respect to the propulsion of the big twins, larger oil vent pipes were installed and the oil tank was new, but the latter would be revised again for the 1939 models.

YEAR:
1938

MANUFACTURER:
Harley-Davidson

MODEL:
UL

ENGINE TYPE:
V-twin

DISPLACEMENT:
74 cubic inches

VALVE TRAIN:
Side valves

CARBURETION:
NA

TRANSMISSION:
Four-speed, hand shift

FRONT SUSPENSION:
Leading link with coil springs

FRONT BRAKE(S):
Drum

REAR SUSPENSION:
Rigid

REAR BRAKE:
Drum

WEIGHT:
NA

FINAL DRIVE:
Chain

OWNER:
Illinois Harley-Davidson

Above: Front fender was bolted to the stationary fork tubes, so it rode far above the wheel to allow clearance over bumps. *Far left:* Warning lights replaced the ammeter and oil-pressure gauges for 1938—a step backward in some regards. *Left:* Horn was prominently displayed below the large round headlight.

1942
HARLEY-DAVIDSON WLA

As the possibility of war became imminent, the U.S. government began to prepare. To fulfill the need for dependable, fuel-efficient transportation, both Harley-Davidson and Indian were approached to provide the military with motorcycles. Both manufacturers came up with their own style of equipment.

The initial offering by Harley-Davidson was the XA, with a new horizontally opposed twin-cylinder engine that had not been built before. After 1000 were produced, the company came up with a better solution.

Harley took its proven performer, the 45-cubic-inch flathead V-twin WL, and tailored it to the needs of the armed forces. A skid plate was fitted beneath the engine, blackout lights were used at the front and rear, and a heavy-duty luggage rack was added to carry a 40-pound field radio. Another common feature was the front-mounted scabbard, which allowed for quick access to the government-issue "Tommy Gun."

YEAR:
1942

MANUFACTURER:
Harley-Davidson

MODEL:
WLA

ENGINE TYPE:
V-twin

DISPLACEMENT:
45 cubic inches

VALVE TRAIN:
Side valves

CARBURETION:
Linkert

TRANSMISSION:
Three-speed, hand shift

FRONT SUSPENSION:
Leading link with coil springs

FRONT BRAKE(S):
Drum

REAR SUSPENSION:
Rigid

REAR BRAKE:
Drum

WEIGHT:
540 pounds

FINAL DRIVE:
Chain

OWNER:
Henry Hardin Family

Top left: Small blackout light on front fender was used when concealment was necessary. A similar taillight is mounted on the rear fender. *Top right:* A metal plate, engraved with pertinent maintenance data, was mounted on top of the fuel tank for quick reference. As a statistical quirk, all WLAs built between 1942 and 1945 were stamped with serial numbers that had a "42" prefix, making it impossible to determine the actual year of manufacture.

1942
INDIAN 841

Produced alongside the tens of thousands of civilian Indians being outfitted for military use during World War II, the 841 was designed specifically for use in the deserts. Penned by Briggs Weaver, Indian's top designer, it represented a radical departure from the typical Indian machine.

The engine of the 841 was a V-twin, but it was mounted perpendicular to normal Indian practice, with the cylinders sticking out the side of the bike into the airstream. To be more cost-effective, many internal components were borrowed from the company's Sport Scout model. Not only was the engine configuration unusual, but it drove the rear wheel via shaft rather than the usual chain—a configuration deemed more suitable for use in the abrasive desert sand.

Much like the Harley-Davidson XA of the same period, only about a thousand 841s were ever built. And due to its late entry, less than fifty were ever pressed into military service. The rest were sold to civilians, most being converted for use on the street, and many can still be found at motorcycle shows across the country.

YEAR:
1942

MANUFACTURER:
Indian

MODEL:
841

ENGINE TYPE:
V-twin

DISPLACEMENT:
45 cubic inches

VALVE TRAIN:
Side valves

CARBURETION:
Linkert

TRANSMISSION:
Four-speed, foot shift

FRONT SUSPENSION:
Girder fork with coil springs and shock absorber

FRONT BRAKE(S):
Drum

REAR SUSPENSION:
Plunger-type with coil springs

REAR BRAKE:
Drum

WEIGHT:
NA

FINAL DRIVE:
Shaft

OWNER:
"Wheels Through Time"
museum

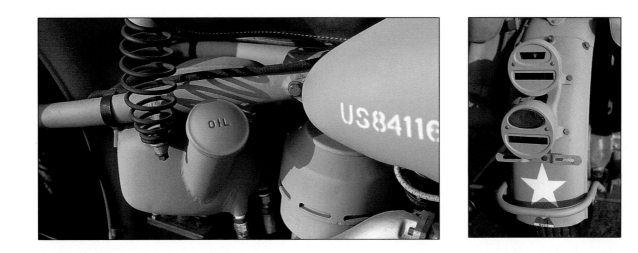

Top left: Military motorcycles were designed with easy maintenance in mind; note the large oil tank beneath the seat and canister-type air filter beneath the tank. *Top right:* Blackout taillight was mounted above regular taillight on rear fender. As with the front blackout headlight, which was mounted above the regular headlight *(above),* the intent was to make the bike harder for the enemy to see at night.

1947
HARLEY-DAVIDSON EL

After its arrival in 1936, Harley's Knucklehead V-twin would continue to power the 61-cubic-inch EL and later the enlarged 74-cubic-inch FL models through 1947. With all the improvements made to the engine over its 11-year production run, many felt the Knucklehead was retired prematurely.

In addition to the EL and FL, there was an ES version with a medium-compression 61-cubic-inch engine that was geared for sidecar use. Also, the WL and UL flathead models were still available in 45- and 74-cubic-inch sizes.

Several changes were made to the final EL models in response to government requirements. The most obvious from a visual standpoint was the larger and brighter "tombstone" taillight. What more people noticed, however, were the new-style mufflers that were quieter than ever before. These pleased not only the government, but also the makers of aftermarket exhaust systems; it seems many riders didn't care to arrive unannounced.

YEAR:
1947

MANUFACTURER:
Harley-Davidson

MODEL:
EL

ENGINE TYPE:
V-twin

DISPLACEMENT:
61 cubic inches

VALVE TRAIN:
Overhead valves

CARBURETION:
Schebler

TRANSMISSION:
Four-speed, hand shift

FRONT SUSPENSION:
Leading link with coil springs

FRONT BRAKE(S):
Drum

REAR SUSPENSION:
Rigid

REAR BRAKE:
Drum

WEIGHT:
NA

FINAL DRIVE:
Chain

OWNER:
David Monahan

In its final year, the EL, with its Knucklehead engine, adopted a quieter muffler *(opposite page)* and brighter "tombstone" taillight *(left)*. Tank-mounted gauge panel *(far left)* changed numerous times over the years, the '47 model featuring simple white-on-black graphics surrounded by a body-colored nacelle. *Center left:* Four-speed hand shifter moved through a "gate" attached to the fuel tank; first was all the way forward, fourth, all the way back.

1947
TRIUMPH SPEED TWIN

In 1936, Edward Turner joined Triumph as its chief designer and general manager. He quickly went to work developing a new lightweight two-cylinder motorcycle, and within two years, the company introduced a landmark machine: the Speed Twin.

First shown in late 1937 and sold as a 1938 model, the Speed Twin's 500-cc engine and four-speed transmission were carried in separate cases—a simple design that would not be duplicated elsewhere for nearly a decade. The combination would be used in several Triumph models over the years, while the Speed Twin itself was the mount of choice for numerous police departments throughout Europe.

The Speed Twin's modern telescopic forks handled suspension chores in front fairly well, but the rigid frame meant that the seat's coil springs were the sole form of "rear" suspension. In 1947 an optional sprung rear hub was offered, and our featured Speed Twin is so equipped. But it turned out to be a disappointment to those who ordered it, for the design allowed only minimal travel while adding a complex inner assembly of springs and related hardware.

YEAR:
1947

MANUFACTURER:
Triumph

MODEL:
Speed Twin

ENGINE TYPE:
Vertical twin

DISPLACEMENT:
500 cc (approx. 30 cubic inches)

VALVE TRAIN:
Overhead valves

CARBURETION:
Amal

TRANSMISSION:
Four-speed, foot shift

FRONT SUSPENSION:
Telescopic

FRONT BRAKE(S):
Drum

REAR SUSPENSION:
Rigid (optional sprung hub)

REAR BRAKE:
Drum

WEIGHT:
350 pounds

FINAL DRIVE:
Chain

OWNER:
Jody Synove

In the mid-Sixties, Triumph joined other manufacturers by combining engines and transmissions into one unit, which resulted in a more compact design. Today, however, "pre-unit" Triumphs are highly coveted, and much sought-after on the collector market. *Left:* Triumph's sprung rear hub, first offered as an option in 1947, afforded about an inch of wheel travel—hardly a substitute for a good swingarm suspension.

1948
HARLEY-DAVIDSON S-125

At the close of World War II, thousands of G.I.s returned to the states hungry for transportation. Many had seen or spent time on the Harley-Davidson WLA military motorcycles in use overseas, and now craved one of their own. With finances being tight for many, Harley decided to build the small, inexpensive S-125 for the masses.

With a single-cylinder two-stroke engine designed by DKW of Germany, this was not the kind of motorcycle most people associated with Harley-Davidson. Yet the company claims that 10,000 were sold in the first seven months of 1947.

Producing only three horsepower, the S-125 had a tough time reaching 55 miles per hour. Though a girder fork with coil spring was used up front, the rear had no suspension other than what was provided by the sprung saddle. But with a three-speed gearbox, foot shift, and hand clutch, the lightweight bike was simple and easy to operate.

Several changes benefitted the little Harley during its 13-year life span. Most notable was a switch to modern "Teleglide" telescopic forks in 1951, and a boost in engine size to 165 ccs in 1954. The following year the bike became known as the Hummer, and it continued with only minor updates through 1959, after which it was dropped in favor of more contemporary designs.

YEAR:
1948

MANUFACTURER:
Harley-Davidson

MODEL:
S-125

ENGINE TYPE:
Vertical single

DISPLACEMENT:
125 cc (approx. 7.6 cubic inches)

VALVE TRAIN:
Two-stroke

CARBURETION:
NA

TRANSMISSION:
Three-speed, foot shift

FRONT SUSPENSION:
Girder fork with coil spring

FRONT BRAKE(S):
Drum

REAR SUSPENSION:
Rigid

REAR BRAKE:
Drum

WEIGHT:
200 pounds

FINAL DRIVE:
Chain

OWNER:
Walter E. Cunny

Though hardly what Harley buyers were used to, the S-125 was an excellent choice as a first bike or around-town runabout, as it was simple, rugged, and easy to ride. Seating for one was accompanied by a handy luggage rack. Horn *(left)* was mounted in a seemingly ineffectual location by the rear wheel.

1948
INDIAN CHIEF

After World War II, the only Indian that returned to production was the big V-twin Chief. Though it was still powered by the old side-valve engine, it exchanged its leaf-spring front suspension for a girder design that had been used on a small number of military Indians built during the war.

In 1948, the Chief received some minor updates. A new instrument panel (still sitting atop the fuel tank) replaced the previous ammeter with a generator light, and speedometers were now provided by Stewart-Warner. More changes showed up at mid-year: In the front forks, needle bearings were replaced by bushings with grease fittings, while the frame cross-member behind the seat post went from a straight section of round tubing to a curved section of rectangular tubing. The Chief pictured is an early '48 model.

Chief buyers could choose from several options in 1948, among them a magneto ignition, high-performance camshaft, four-speed gearbox (in place of the standard three-speed), and even a reverse gear. In addition, Turquoise joined the existing rainbow of color choices.

YEAR:
1948

MANUFACTURER:
Indian

MODEL:
Chief

ENGINE TYPE:
V-twin

DISPLACEMENT:
74 cubic inches

VALVE TRAIN:
Side valves

CARBURETION:
Linkert

TRANSMISSION:
Three-speed, hand shift (four-speed and reverse gear optional)

FRONT SUSPENSION:
Girder fork with coil springs

FRONT BRAKE(S):
Drum

REAR SUSPENSION:
Plunger-type with coil springs

REAR BRAKE:
Drum

WEIGHT:
550 pounds

FINAL DRIVE:
Chain

OWNER:
Vance Clute

Left: Changes to the '48 Chief included a sleeker-looking exhaust system, which joined the front and rear headers into a single unit that clamped directly to the muffler. *Above:* Speedometer, mounted on top of the fuel tank, was as classy as it was functional.

1949
HARLEY-DAVIDSON FL

In 1948, Harley-Davidson replaced the venerable Knucklehead motor in its large FL models with the new, improved "Panhead" powerplant. Featuring aluminum alloy cylinder heads, heat dissipation was greatly improved and a new rocker-arm design helped eliminate noise from the tappets.

The big news for 1949 was the introduction of "Hydra Glide" front forks. Replacing the former leading-link forks, Hydra Glide was a modern telescopic design that provided a much higher level of riding comfort. However, the frame still lacked any form of rear suspension; that would take another few years to develop.

The 1949 FL was not only more comfortable to ride, but also easier to stop due to a larger front brake. Though by this time many motorcycles (mostly smaller ones) were adopting foot-shift transmissions, that too was some time off for the big FL series, which still made use of a hand shifter and foot clutch.

YEAR:
1949

MANUFACTURER:
Harley-Davidson

MODEL:
FL

ENGINE TYPE:
V-twin

DISPLACEMENT:
74 cubic inches

VALVE TRAIN:
Overhead valves

CARBURETION:
Schebler

TRANSMISSION:
Four-speed, hand shift

FRONT SUSPENSION:
Telescopic

FRONT BRAKE(S):
Drum

REAR SUSPENSION:
Rigid

REAR BRAKE:
Drum

WEIGHT:
NA

FINAL DRIVE:
Chain

OWNER:
Marvin Bredemeir

Above: When the Hydra Glide first appeared in 1949, the aluminum trim on the top of the fork tubes was not stamped with the Hydra Glide logo; this would not be added until later in the model year. *Right:* Though the shape of the gauge panel remained the same for years, colors used on the speedometer's face changed frequently. *Far right:* Harleys were getting custom touches way back in the Forties: note the chrome taillight housing flanked by chrome speedlines and underlined with a chrome gravel shield.

1951
TRIUMPH T100

The T100 made its first appearance in 1939 and was regarded as one of Edward Turner's best efforts. Considered to be a high-performance version of the Speed Twin line, the T100 got its name from a top speed that approached 100 mph.

Like the Speed Twin, the T100 had a separate transmission and engine, the latter with an all-iron block and head until 1951. At that time, more tightly finned cylinders were capped with new light-alloy heads.

Front suspension on the T100 was telescopic, and the rear wheel was carried on a sprung hub. Intended as a substitute for "real" rear suspension, the sprung hub allowed for only one inch of wheel travel, and due to its complexity, was not well received.

Early T100s were built with a tank-mounted instrument panel. Since this location forced the rider to take his eyes off the road to scan the display, it was later moved to the top of the headlight nacelle for reasons of safety, and the oil-pressure gauge was deleted. The vacancy on the tank was filled with a chrome package shelf.

The T100 seen here has been fitted with the Triumph factory race kit. The headlight has been replaced by a number plate, while a lay-down pad is mounted where the package shelf used to be.

YEAR:
1951

MANUFACTURER:
Triumph

MODEL:
T100

ENGINE TYPE:
Vertical twin

DISPLACEMENT:
498 cc (approx. 30 cubic inches)

VALVE TRAIN:
Overhead valves

CARBURETION:
Amal

TRANSMISSION:
Four-speed, foot shift

FRONT SUSPENSION:
Telescopic

FRONT BRAKE(S):
Drum

REAR SUSPENSION:
Sprung hub

REAR BRAKE:
Drum

WEIGHT:
320 pounds

FINAL DRIVE:
Chain

OWNER:
Bob Baumgartner

Outfitted for racing, this T100 wears a number plate in place of a headlight, and a chest pad on top of the tank where a luggage rack would normally reside. *Left:* A thumbwheel allows quick adjustment of the rear brake. *Below:* A tachometer is fitted in a recess of the headlight nacelle, which otherwise would carry a speedometer.

1951
VINCENT HRD SERIES B RAPIDE

After purchasing the HRD company in 1928, Philip Vincent applied the name to his own line of motorcycles. As an inventor and engineer, Mr. Vincent produced some very innovative designs during his career, and bikes carrying the Vincent HRD logo were known for their quality construction—and high prices. It was the latter that would lead to the company's demise in 1955.

Vincent's first models were powered by engines produced by the JAP company (as were many other motorcycles of the era), and sported rear suspensions—unusual for the day. But in 1935 the company introduced its own engine, a 500-cc overhead-valve single, and V-twins soon followed.

The early V-twin engine, mounted in a motorcycle called the Series A 1000, gained the nickname "plumber's nightmare" due to its spaghetti-like web of external oil lines. After World War II, the Series B Rapide appeared with a cleaner design. The new engine was a 50-degree V-twin that doubled as a structural frame member; gone were the front and rear down tubes of older models. Postwar Vincents therefore looked a bit odd, as though all the individual components were bolted to each other rather than to a skeletal frame—which, in essence, they were.

In 1949, a tuned, high-performance version of the Rapide joined the line. Called the Series C Black Shadow, it was even faster than the Rapide, and today is one of the most coveted classic motorcycles in the world.

YEAR:
1951

MANUFACTURER:
Vincent HRD

MODEL:
Series B Rapide

ENGINE TYPE:
V-twin

DISPLACEMENT:
998 cc (approx. 61 cubic inches)

VALVE TRAIN:
Overhead valves

CARBURETION:
Amal

TRANSMISSION:
Four-speed, foot shift

FRONT SUSPENSION:
Girder fork with coil-over shock

FRONT BRAKE(S):
Drum

REAR SUSPENSION:
Triangulated swingarm with coil-over shocks

REAR BRAKE:
Drum

WEIGHT:
455 pounds

FINAL DRIVE:
Chain

OWNER:
Hugh Hall

With the engine as a major supporting member, Vincents had virtually no frame. *Top:* Note coil-over shocks mounted beneath the seat. *Left:* In the states, many thought "H.R.D." stood for "Harley R. Davidson," and that the Vincent, with its classic American V-twin engine, was associated with Harley-Davidson. Not so. *Above:* The Rapide had polished engine cases, whereas the high-performance Black Shadow variant had black cases.

1952
TRIUMPH THUNDERBIRD

As is often the case, a foreign manufacturer that exports to the U.S. has to listen carefully to the changing demands of the marketplace. And that's just what Triumph did when it released the 6T in 1950.

While the company's offerings were generally well received in postwar America, there was a cry for more power from those accustomed to large-displacement Indians and Harley-Davidsons. And though the 6T's 650-cc engine was barely half the size of the thunderous V-twins of those rivals, it was at least a step in the right direction.

Triumph's popular Speed Twin was the basis for the 6T, and their engines looked the same from the outside. But it was what was inside that made the difference: some minor modifications and an extra 150 ccs of displacement netted eight more horsepower, raising the total to 34.

Also new was the styling. A monotone paint scheme bathed frame, tanks, forks, fenders, and even wheel rims in the same color, while new badges and a luggage rack graced the fuel tank.

As was Triumph's custom, the 6T was given a "stage name" in addition to its alpha-numeric designation, and Thunderbird became the chosen moniker—this, of course, years before Ford's two-seat sports car took on the same name. One can't help but think that today, this "coincidence" would have evoked some sort of legal action.

YEAR:
1952

MANUFACTURER:
Triumph

MODEL:
Thunderbird

ENGINE TYPE:
Vertical twin

DISPLACEMENT:
650 cc (approx. 40 cubic inches)

VALVE TRAIN:
Overhead valves

CARBURETION:
S.U.

TRANSMISSION:
Four-speed, foot shift

FRONT SUSPENSION:
Telescopic

FRONT BRAKE(S):
Drum

REAR SUSPENSION:
Sprung hub

REAR BRAKE:
Drum

WEIGHT:
340 pounds

FINAL DRIVE:
Chain

OWNER:
Bob Baumgartner

A Triumph Thunderbird was Marlon Brando's mount in the 1954 film, *The Wild One*. *Opposite page:* Though modern telescopic forks supported the front end, some Triumphs of this period used a rigid rear frame with a sprung hub on the rear wheel. The sprung hub was a complex mechanical arrangement that only allowed about one inch of wheel travel—hardly worth the effort. *Above right:* Pre-unit Triumphs, in which the engine and transmission were housed in separate cases, had an oil tank mounted beneath the seat. The transmission is below the oil tank.

1953
INDIAN CHIEF

The first Indian Chief was rolled out in 1922. Designed by Charles Franklin, it has become the most recognized of all Indian models.

Though Indian enjoyed a long and rich history, by 1952, the company found itself in dire straits. With little money for product improvements, only minor alterations were made to the 1952 models, with even fewer changes made for '53.

Modern telescopic forks had been added to the Chief in 1950, when the 74-cubic-inch V-twin was enlarged to 80 cubic inches. Foot shift was also made available that year, though it wouldn't become a regular production item until 1951.

For 1952, a solid-mounted seat replaced the former sprung saddle, and a protective shield was mounted over the distributor. At the front end, a lower-profile tire gave the Chief a more manageable ride height, and the fender had a thinner profile.

In its final year, the headlight high/low switch was moved to the floorboard, but otherwise the Chief carried on with few changes. It also carried on alone; other Indian models had already been discontinued.

According to factory records, 700 Chiefs were built in 1952, while only 600 were completed in 1953. After that, the Chief—and Indian along with it—was relegated to history, leaving Harley-Davidson as the sole surviving American motorcycle manufacturer.

YEAR:
1953

MANUFACTURER:
Indian

MODEL:
Chief

ENGINE TYPE:
V-twin

DISPLACEMENT:
80 cubic inches

VALVE TRAIN:
Side valves

CARBURETION:
Linkert

TRANSMISSION:
Three-speed, hand shift
(foot shift optional)

FRONT SUSPENSION:
Telescopic

FRONT BRAKE(S):
Drum

REAR SUSPENSION:
Plunger-type with coil springs

REAR BRAKE:
Drum

WEIGHT:
570 pounds

FINAL DRIVE:
Chain

OWNER:
Jim Anderson

Left: By 1953, the Chief was loaded down with sheetmetal bodywork, the latest addition being a cowling that was mounted behind the headlight. *Bottom left:* Indian enlarged its traditional 74-cubic-inch V-twin to 80 cubic inches in 1950, and those models received a signifying decal on their fuel tanks. Chrome dominated the rider's view *(bottom right)*, and as evidenced by the shift knob in the lower left corner, the original buyer of this machine opted for the traditional hand shift over the optional foot shift that had been available since 1950.

1953
TRIUMPH DRAG BIKE

Triumph had long been renowned for building a solid vertical-twin engine, and the company's larger bikes were fairly quick for their time. Of course, some folks contended that the bikes were not quick enough, and many were modified for various racing events. In addition to dirt track and road racing, Triumphs could also be terrors on the drag strip.

Our featured bike was built around a 650-cc engine out of a 1953 Triumph Thunderbird. The displacement was bumped to 800 ccs with a kit from Routt, which also upped the compression ratio to 10.5:1. Dual racing carbs with velocity stacks replaced the stock Amal, and mufflers were removed to decrease back pressure.

An early Triumph frame made a perfect home for the modified powerplant, though the swingarm was replaced with solid struts and the front end was lowered. Adding a fat M & H slick to the rear insured that power would get to the ground, while a peanut tank and bikini fairing provided the finishing touches.

Considering that this bike was built from such vintage pieces, it's surprising that it can run down the quarter-mile in less than 12 seconds—and put a smile on your face that will last much longer.

YEAR:
1953

MANUFACTURER:
Triumph

MODEL:
Modified Thunderbird

ENGINE TYPE:
V-twin

DISPLACEMENT:
800 cc (approx. 49 cubic inches)

VALVE TRAIN:
Overhead valves

CARBURETION:
NA

TRANSMISSION:
Four-speed, foot shift

FRONT SUSPENSION:
Telescopic

FRONT BRAKE(S):
Drum

REAR SUSPENSION:
Rigid

REAR BRAKE:
Drum

WEIGHT:
280 pounds

FINAL DRIVE:
Chain

OWNER:
Bob Baumgartner

Even though Harleys offered more displacement, Triumphs were often chosen for racing due to their lighter weight and higher-revving engines. *Far left:* "Heel-and-toe" shift lever was used to facilitate quicker gear changes. *Left:* Though the purpose of a dragster is to go, at about the end of the strip, one needs to think about stopping. Having this ventilated drum brake up front was no doubt a comfort.

1954
AJS 16M

The Stevens brothers began their business by building engines for use in the frames of other manufacturers. In 1911, the initials of the oldest brother, Albert John Stevens, would appear on their first complete motorcycle. AJS took home several trophies in the early days of TT racing, and this experience helped its sales for many years.

AJS continued as an independent manufacturer until 1931, when financial woes forced it to join forces with the Matchless company. Although both lines were labeled differently, AJS and Matchless became synonymous in name and construction. Being outfitted with different trim did little to separate the two brands.

The 16M was the first postwar AJS to be released. Its mechanical roots ran back to the models of 1935, though improvements had been implemented in the intervening years. The 16M breathed through a larger Amal carb in 1954, and also had a new automatic ignition-advance mechanism that made riding more pleasant. To make room for this revision, a new side cover was installed, easily identified by a hump in its surface.

Much like the early Fords, AJS cycles were always finished in black with gold striping, while their Matchless siblings were trimmed with silver.

YEAR:
1954

MANUFACTURER:
AJS

MODEL:
16M

ENGINE TYPE:
Vertical single

DISPLACEMENT:
348 cc (approx. 21 cubic inches)

VALVE TRAIN:
Overhead valves

CARBURETION:
Amal

TRANSMISSION:
Four-speed, foot shift

FRONT SUSPENSION:
Telescopic

FRONT BRAKE(S):
Drum

REAR SUSPENSION:
Swingarm with coil-over shocks

REAR BRAKE:
Drum

WEIGHT:
NA

FINAL DRIVE:
Chain

OWNER:
John Murphy

Far left: Small cap-like protrusion in left-side engine cover ahead of the footpeg housed the new-for-'54 automatic ignition advance. Though AJS and Matchless machines were virtually identical mechanically, AJS versions had distinct generator-drive covers *(left)* and wore gold trim rather than silver *(below).*

1954
HARLEY-DAVIDSON FLF

For all the ballyhoo surrounding the 50th anniversary of Harley-Davidson, not much was really changed on the FL models. The Panhead engine would not receive any major revisions until 1955, and all previous changes were carried into the 1954 models.

The FLF was the standard compression, foot-shift version of the 74-cubic-inch Harleys. Those that requested the optional hand shift were aided by a helper spring to overcome the tension of the latest clutch.

In addition to the commemorative front fender badge, the 50th Anniversary FLs were shown with a new trumpet-style horn. This FLF is finished in Anniversary Yellow paint and is also fitted with the optional color-matched hand grips and kick-start pedal. Other paint choices, including two-tones (with the tank and fenders in different colors), were also available.

FL models accounted for nearly half of all Harleys sold in 1954. Total sales were down from the previous year, even though arch-rival Indian had closed its doors at the end of 1953—just after its 50th anniversary. Harley sales wouldn't rebound until 1957, with the introduction of the famed Sportster.

YEAR:
1954

MANUFACTURER:
Harley-Davidson

MODEL:
FLF

ENGINE TYPE:
V-twin

DISPLACEMENT:
74 cubic inches

VALVE TRAIN:
Overhead valves

CARBURETION:
NA

TRANSMISSION:
Four-speed, foot shift

FRONT SUSPENSION:
Telescopic

FRONT BRAKE(S):
Drum

REAR SUSPENSION:
Rigid

REAR BRAKE:
Drum

WEIGHT:
NA

FINAL DRIVE:
Chain

OWNER:
John Archacki

Far left: Commemorative front fender badge celebrated Harley's Golden Anniversary. *Left:* Speedometer color schemes changed almost yearly; for '54, it was green-on-black with gold center. *Below:* Between the Anniversary Yellow paint and liberal application of chrome, this '54 FLF really stands out in a crowd.

1956
SIMPLEX AUTOMATIC

The Simplex Automatic was designed and built in the U.S. There were several other manufacturers that used the Simplex name, but they hailed from Holland, Italy, and England.

Built in New Orleans, Louisiana, the Simplex was the brainchild of Mr. Paul Treen, who started the company in the late Twenties with a $25 investment. A draftsman by trade and inventor by nature, the Simplex was a natural extension of his abilities and vision. Surprisingly, it was the only motorcycle ever built in the southern part of the country.

The first Simplex arrived in 1935, and as the name implied, was built with simplicity in mind. Its 125-cc engine powered the rear wheel through a direct-drive arrangement, eliminating the complexity (and expense) of a transmission and clutch.

Later models, however, added more features. The Simplex Automatic shown here was fitted with a unique automatic transmission and torque converter combination. Furthermore, the two-stroke engine featured a rotary valve that was quite unusual for the period. Light weight and efficient design combined to return a claimed 100 mpg.

Simplex cycles were built until 1960. During their life span, new models and revisions were frequent due to Mr. Treens' tireless efforts to improve on his simple motorcycle design. The company continued to build go-carts for several years after motorcycle production was halted.

YEAR:
1956

MANUFACTURER:
Simplex

MODEL:
Automatic

ENGINE TYPE:
Vertical single

DISPLACEMENT:
125 cc (approx. 8 cubic inches)

VALVE TRAIN:
Two-stroke

CARBURETION:
Tillottson

TRANSMISSION:
Automatic

FRONT SUSPENSION:
Leading link with coil springs

FRONT BRAKE(S):
None

REAR SUSPENSION:
Rigid

REAR BRAKE:
Drum

WEIGHT:
NA

FINAL DRIVE:
Belt

OWNER:
Jim, Jeff, and Kevin Minnis

In the Simplex Automatic, power was routed through an automatic clutch to a variable transmission, and then on to the rear wheel. Rather than a chain or plain belt, the Simplex used "linked" leather belts to transfer driving forces. *Left:* Evidently, top speed was insufficient to warrant the inclusion of a speedometer.

1957
ARIEL 4G MK II

During the 1920s, Ariel's Edward Turner had dreams of changing the world of motorcycling. For many years, the twin-cylinder engine was the powerplant of choice, but Edward longed for more. Envisioning a four-cylinder engine that would fit neatly into a typical frame, he devised the unusual "square four" design. It used two crankshafts geared together and four cylinders arranged in a square pattern, with a pair of pistons tied to each crankshaft.

Displacing 500 ccs, the first Ariel Square Four appeared in 1931, venting its exhaust through only two pipes. The four was enlarged to 600 ccs in 1932, and then to 1000 ccs in 1936. In 1953, the Mk II version appeared, carrying a four-pipe exhaust system and an alloy block in place of the previous iron version.

Square Four production continued through the 1950s, after which Ariel concentrated on medium-displacement two-strokes that were a cross between a scooter and a motorcycle. But like many other British manufacturers, Ariel fell on hard times during the Sixties, and was out of the motorcycle trade entirely by 1970.

YEAR:
1957

MANUFACTURER:
Ariel

MODEL:
4G Mk II

ENGINE TYPE:
Square four

DISPLACEMENT:
1000 cc (approx. 61 cubic inches)

VALVE TRAIN:
Overhead valves

CARBURETION:
SU

TRANSMISSION:
Four-speed, foot shift

FRONT SUSPENSION:
Telescopic

FRONT BRAKE(S):
Drum

REAR SUSPENSION:
Plunger-type with coil springs

REAR BRAKE:
Drum

WEIGHT:
465 pounds

FINAL DRIVE:
Chain

OWNER:
R. B. McClean

Above: Ariel's original Square Four, sometimes referred to as the "Squariel," used a girder fork, but switched to a modern telescopic design in 1946. Other changes over the years included the addition of plunger-type rear suspension. Instruments were originally mounted on top of the fuel tank, but were later moved to the top of the steering head, and, in the mid-Fifties, to the top of the headlight nacelle *(left)*.

1959
ARIEL LEADER

Prior to the unveiling of the Leader, Ariel had been known for its four-stroke singles, twins, and the unique Square Four. But after exhaustive market research, the company decided it was time to change direction.

What appeared in July of 1958 was a combination of several new technologies for Ariel, primarily the use of a two-stroke engine, pressed-steel frame, and odd-looking trailing-link front forks. The enclosed styling allowed for a chassis structure that stored fuel beneath the seat, while the "tank" served as a convenient storage area.

One of the most interesting aspects of the Leader was the long list of options available. As a result, few of the 22,000 produced were exactly the same. Color choices included Oriental Blue or Cherry Red with Admiral Gray accents, and the model featured sports the optional side bags and rear luggage rack.

YEAR:
1959

MANUFACTURER:
Ariel

MODEL:
Leader

ENGINE TYPE:
V-twin

DISPLACEMENT:
247 cc (approx. 15 cubic inches)

VALVE TRAIN:
Two-stroke

CARBURETION:
Amal

TRANSMISSION:
Four-speed, foot shift

FRONT SUSPENSION:
Trailing link with coil springs

FRONT BRAKE(S):
Drum

REAR SUSPENSION:
Swingarm with coil-over shocks

REAR BRAKE:
Drum

WEIGHT:
NA

FINAL DRIVE:
Chain

OWNER:
John Murphy

Above: Despite its rather odd looks, the Leader was a functional vehicle that offered many useful features and options. The enclosed body made cleaning a snap, and the full fairing and windshield made cool-weather riding more bearable. *Top right:* Instrument panel included a speedometer, ammeter, and of all things, a clock. *Bottom right:* Optional luggage rack and side bags add carrying capacity. Note wild paisley seat cover.

1959
HARLEY-DAVIDSON FL

Harley-Davidson motorcycles had proven their mettle throughout the company's first 50 years of production. Action in two world wars confirmed their reliability, and for many years, both the federal government and local municipalities rode Harley-Davidsons exclusively. Of course, they were also wildly popular in the private sector.

Thousands of Harley-Davidsons have been put to use keeping the peace in cities across America, police departments large and small recognizing the value of having two-wheeled patrol units on their forces.

Missing out on the exciting life led by siblings in military and law-enforcement duty, this 1959 FL served as a funeral escort by the Franklin County Sheriffs Department in Ohio. Since high-speed chases were not in the job description, the FL retains its hand shift lever, whereas other departments opted for foot-shifting versions. But that just makes this silver FL all the more rare—and desirable.

YEAR:
1959

MANUFACTURER:
Harley-Davidson

MODEL:
FL

ENGINE TYPE:
V-twin

DISPLACEMENT:
74 cubic inches

VALVE TRAIN:
Overhead valves

CARBURETION:
NA

TRANSMISSION:
Four-speed, hand shift
(foot shift available)

FRONT SUSPENSION:
Telescopic

FRONT BRAKE(S):
Drum

REAR SUSPENSION:
Swingarm with coil-over shocks

REAR BRAKE:
Drum

WEIGHT:
NA

FINAL DRIVE:
Chain

OWNER:
Al and Pat Doerman

Far left: Harley continually changed speedometer colors, this '59 wearing teal numbers on a blue background. *Left:* Hand-shift Harleys were on the decline by this time, most being ordered with foot shift. Hand-shift models came with a foot-activated clutch; pushing down on the front pad disengaged the clutch, pushing down on the rear pad engaged it.

1959
ROYAL ENFIELD INDIAN

In a desperate attempt to increase floor traffic and boost sales, Indian dealers began to carry several makes of British motorcycles alongside their own. As the supplier of the British motorcycles, Brockhouse Ltd. also provided financing to the ailing concern. By 1950, the entire situation had worsened and Brockhouse took control of Indian.

To maintain a flow of "Indian" machines, Brockhouse began badging Royal Enfields as Indians. This 250-cc single was brought over to serve as an entry-level model, the tank bearing a large Indian badge backed by a gleaming chrome panel. Single-cylinder Indians had been sold before, so the move was not without precedent.

Several Royal Enfield models adopted Indian badges after Indian itself went under. But there were few buyers in the U.S., and this charade didn't last much past the Sixties.

YEAR:
1959

MANUFACTURER:
Royal Enfield

MODEL:
Indian

ENGINE TYPE:
Vertical single

DISPLACEMENT:
248 cc (approx. 15 cubic inches)

VALVE TRAIN:
Overhead valves

CARBURETION:
NA

TRANSMISSION:
Four-speed, foot shift

FRONT SUSPENSION:
Telescopic

FRONT BRAKE(S):
Drum

REAR SUSPENSION:
Swingarm with coil-over shocks

REAR BRAKE:
Drum

WEIGHT:
NA

FINAL DRIVE:
Chain

OWNER:
R. B. McClean

The single-cylinder Royal Enfield Indian is a good example of motorcycle simplicity. A single-downtube frame supported the 250-cc engine, and suspension pieces were off-the-shelf Royal Enfield components. Front and rear drum brakes were perfectly adequate to slow the lightweight machine.

1959
TRIUMPH 3TA

The non-riding public in Britain often looked at motorcycles as being the transportation of choice of the local ruffians. In an effort to appeal to a more genteel audience, Triumph designed the 3TA to look different than the usual motorcycle.

By enveloping the rear wheel in a "bathtub," as it became to be known, Triumph went for a clean, uncluttered look. To augment the rear enclosure, the front fender was given a graceful flare and sat beneath an aviation-style headlight nacelle. First shown in 1957, the 3TA was smooth and scooter-like, yet the public's response was not positive. Most of those who took delivery of the 3TA removed the rear wheel enclosure and reverted to a traditional fender, as shown here.

"The 21," as it was referred to in the U.S., was powered by a 349-cc engine of unit construction. As ungainly as it looked, the 3TA proved to be a competitive cycle, its light weight giving it an advantage over many more-powerful machines.

YEAR:
1959

MANUFACTURER:
Triumph

MODEL:
3TA

ENGINE TYPE:
Vertical twin

DISPLACEMENT:
348 cc (approx. 21 cubic inches)

VALVE TRAIN:
Overhead valves

CARBURETION:
Amal

TRANSMISSION:
Four-speed, foot shift

FRONT SUSPENSION:
Telescopic

FRONT BRAKE(S):
Drum

REAR SUSPENSION:
Swingarm with coil-over shocks

REAR BRAKE:
Drum

WEIGHT:
345 pounds

FINAL DRIVE:
Chain

OWNER:
Jim, Jeff, and Kevin Minnis

Above and left: Smooth, flowing contours of headlight nacelle and front fender were intended to give the 3TA a "friendlier" appearance. Though it was never particularly popular with buyers, the 3TA led to the development of other Triumph models, including touring and sport machines.

1961
MATCHLESS G-12

The Collier brothers began building motorcycles in 1899, making them one of the oldest manufacturers on record. Their first machines were assembled using engines from a variety of companies, but later models carried engines of Matchless's own design. In order to prove the abilities of their products, the Collier boys raced their creations, winning the first Isle of Man TT (Tourist Trophy) race in 1907.

With Khaki enamel applied to all of the fuel tanks, color was not an option—but a staggering array of available engines were. Offering both side- and overhead-valve powerplants with displacements ranging from 246 ccs up to 990 ccs, buyers could easily tailor a Matchless to suit their needs.

With the industry in a state of turmoil during the Thirties, Matchless bought out AJS and formed Associated Motor Cycles (AMC). After the war, Norton joined AMC.

The 1961 G-12 pictured is a 650-cc vertical twin that competed against similar Triumph and BSA models of the period and, at least in terms of sales, lost. AMC was restructured in 1966, and afterward only the Norton name returned to the marketplace.

YEAR:
1961

MANUFACTURER:
Matchless

MODEL:
G-12

ENGINE TYPE:
Vertical twin

DISPLACEMENT:
650 cc (approx. 40 cubic inches)

VALVE TRAIN:
Overhead valves

CARBURETION:
Amal

TRANSMISSION:
Four-speed, foot shift

FRONT SUSPENSION:
Telescopic

FRONT BRAKE(S):
Drum

REAR SUSPENSION:
Swingarm with coil-over shocks

REAR BRAKE:
Drum

WEIGHT:
NA

FINAL DRIVE:
Chain

OWNER:
Ralph and Nancy Dam

After Matchless bought out AJS in the early Thirties, motorcycles continued to be offered under both names, though the bikes themselves were nearly identical except for badging. The Matchless name shows up only in fine print on the oil tank *(left)*, while other badges feature Matchless's winged-M logo.

1961
VELOCETTE VENOM

Velocette was founded in 1904 under the name Veloce. Its first motorcycles were powered by four-stroke engines, but when the company switched to two-strokes in 1913, the name was changed to Velocette. Though four-strokes reappeared in the Twenties, the company name was retained.

When most rivals added large-displacement twins to their lineups, Velocette stuck with vertical singles. One exception was the LE, introduced in 1949, a small, scooter-like machine powered by a 200-cc, horizontally opposed flathead twin. It was a practical mount but never very popular, though Velocette spent plenty trying to make it so.

The Venom was introduced in the late Fifties, and while it was a capable sporting machine, it was overshadowed in the marketplace by various British twins. Its 500-cc engine produced a respectable 36 horsepower, enough to propel the Venom to near 100 mph. A Venom equipped with the "Clubman" option could top the century mark.

In the mid-Sixties the Thruxton Venom appeared, named after a popular racing circuit. But despite an updated appearance and a bit more power, it couldn't save Velocette, and the company folded in 1968.

YEAR:
1961

MANUFACTURER:
Velocette

MODEL:
Venom

ENGINE TYPE:
Vertical single

DISPLACEMENT:
500 cc (approx. 30 cubic inches)

VALVE TRAIN:
Overhead cam

CARBURETION:
Amal

TRANSMISSION:
Four-speed, foot shift

FRONT SUSPENSION:
Telescopic

FRONT BRAKE(S):
Drum

REAR SUSPENSION:
Swingarm with coil-over shocks

REAR BRAKE:
Drum

WEIGHT:
400 pounds

FINAL DRIVE:
Chain

OWNER:
R. B. McClean

Velocettes ran with large-displacement vertical singles while most rivals boasted twins. Nonetheless, later models were impressively fast, some able to top 100 mph. *Opposite page:* Left side of engine was shrouded with black-painted covers, but right side *(above)* boasted beautiful castings. Note "fishtail" muffler, common on many bikes of the era. Rear suspension could be adjusted to compensate for a passenger's weight by altering the top mounting point of the coil-over shocks—an unusual and useful feature. Bullet headlight housing *(left)*, containing light switch, ammeter, and speedometer, was considered "sleek" in its day.

1962
BSA A65 STAR

BSA (Birmingham Small Arms) started off building firearms, but in the early 1900s began producing motorcycle parts that were sold to other manufacturers, and later its own motorcycles.

After World War II, BSA brought out the A7 and A10 vertical twins, displacing 500- and 650-ccs respectively. Both carried engines and transmissions in separate cases. In 1962, they were redesigned with "unit" construction, having the engine and transmission in one case. The new models were designated the A50 and A65, again displacing 500 and 650 ccs.

The A65 Star was the more popular of the two models and was loaded with new features. The cylinder head was now made of alloy, which kept the twin cooler. An alloy intake manifold fed both cylinders through a single Amal carburetor. The A10's dynamo was replaced with a six-volt alternator accompanied by twin ignition coils.

YEAR:
1962

MANUFACTURER:
BSA

MODEL:
A65 Star

ENGINE TYPE:
Vertical twin

DISPLACEMENT:
650 cc (approx. 40 cubic inches)

VALVE TRAIN:
Overhead valves

CARBURETION:
Amal

TRANSMISSION:
Four-speed, foot shift

FRONT SUSPENSION:
Telescopic

FRONT BRAKE(S):
Drum

REAR SUSPENSION:
Swingarm with coil-over shocks

REAR BRAKE:
Drum

WEIGHT:
NA

FINAL DRIVE:
Chain

OWNER:
Ted Moran

Along with its new "unit" engine and transmission for 1962, the Star got a revised frame. *Far left:* There was also a new headlight nacelle, which now housed the speedometer and ammeter, along with a steering damper and fork lock. Options included a safety bar and enclosed drive chain, both of which were fitted to the bike pictured.

1962
NORTON MANX

Norton began building motorcycles in 1902, when the industry was in its infancy. Five years later, a Norton won the first Isle of Man race, and thus began a long history of competition successes for the British company.

The Manx model that debuted in 1946 was a stripped-down, purpose-built racer powered by a 500-cc single-cylinder engine. Improvements were made on a continual basis, but in 1950 a major change took place when the famous "featherbed" frame was introduced. The design and construction technique made this frame one of the strongest ever produced, and while it was initially used only on factory racers, in 1951 availability was expanded to include standard racing models purchased by privateers.

By 1960, the Norton Manx had reached the pinnacle of its racing career, yet production was officially discontinued the following year. A few 1962 models were assembled using leftover parts, and these last-of-the-breed racers received a new front hub and larger brakes.

Afterward, Norton was consolidated into Associated Motor Cycles (AMC), and though the company continued to prosper in the street-bike market—at least for a while—it would never again experience the kind of racing success it had enjoyed with the Manx.

YEAR:
1962

MANUFACTURER:
Norton

MODEL:
Manx

ENGINE TYPE:
Vertical single

DISPLACEMENT:
500 cc (approx. 30 cubic inches)

VALVE TRAIN:
Overhead cam

CARBURETION:
NA

TRANSMISSION:
Four-speed, foot shift

FRONT SUSPENSION:
Telescopic

FRONT BRAKE(S):
Drum

REAR SUSPENSION:
Swingarm with coil-over shock

REAR BRAKE:
Drum

WEIGHT:
NA

FINAL DRIVE:
Chain

OWNER:
Bley USA

Left and bottom left: One of the most successful factory racers ever built, the Manx was a competitive mount for nearly two decades. Single overhead cam was shaft-driven, and primary chain and dry clutch ran exposed. *Below:* Racers need only know how fast the engine is going—not how fast the bike is going. Lone tachometer indicates a 7200-rpm redline.

1964
HARLEY-DAVIDSON FLH

Harley's big FL-series bikes received numerous updates over the years. Most notable were the replacement of the venerable Knucklehead engine with the Panhead in 1948, adoption of telescopic front forks on the Hydra Glide of 1949, and the addition of rear suspension on the Duo-Glide in 1958. The last was a rather long-awaited improvement; the big Indians had plunger-type rear suspension since the early Forties, so Harley was nearly twenty years behind with this development.

By this time, styling accessories were becoming more prevalent. Replete with half-tinted windshield, chrome headlight cover, dual fish-tail mufflers, chrome handrail, and accessory dual spotlights and Buddy seat, this 1964 FLH is ready to wow 'em at the local drive-in.

YEAR:
1964

MANUFACTURER:
Harley-Davidson

MODEL:
FLH

ENGINE TYPE:
V-twin

DISPLACEMENT:
74 cubic inches

VALVE TRAIN:
Overhead valve

CARBURETION:
Schebler

TRANSMISSION:
Four-speed, foot shift
(hand shift optional)

FRONT SUSPENSION:
Telescopic

FRONT BRAKE(S):
Drum

REAR SUSPENSION:
Swingarm with coil-over shocks

REAR BRAKE:
Drum

WEIGHT
580 pounds

FINAL DRIVE:
Chain

OWNER:
John Archacki

Unlike Indian, which used a plunger-type rear suspension system, Harley-Davidson adopted a conventional swingarm with coil-over shocks for its 1958 Duo-Glide. But Harley enclosed the shocks in chrome sleeves, giving them a custom appearance that was more in keeping with the company's image. *Left:* Tank-mounted instrument housing was protected by a nifty chromed guard rail.

1964
TRIUMPH TIGER CUB

Under the direction of Edward Turner, Triumph ceased production of single-cylinder models in 1939 to concentrate on twins. As time went on, however, the market once again called for a small, lightweight motorcycle, and Triumph obliged with the Terrier in 1952. Powered by a 149-cc four-stroke single, the Terrier proved a success—largely because its competitors were mostly two-stroke machines that seemed less refined.

An upgrade of the Terrier appeared in 1954 as the Cub, with a 10-horsepower 200-cc engine. Triumph offered the models concurrently, hoping that buyers would start with a Terrier and "move up" to a Cub.

Both the Terrier and Cub originally had plunger-type rear suspensions, but were switched over to conventional swingarms in 1957. They also had unit-construction engines, with the engine and gearbox carried in the same case; Triumph's twins of the day had the engine and gearbox in separate cases.

By 1964 the Cub had reached the pinnacle of its development, changing little thereafter. Once again the market was embracing larger, twin-cylinder motorcycles, and the Cub was retired after 1968.

YEAR:
1964

MANUFACTURER:
Triumph

MODEL:
Tiger Cub

ENGINE TYPE:
Vertical single

DISPLACEMENT:
200 cc (approx. 12 cubic inches)

VALVE TRAIN:
Overhead valves

CARBURETION:
Amal

TRANSMISSION:
Four-speed, foot shift

FRONT SUSPENSION:
Telescopic

FRONT BRAKE(S):
Drum

REAR SUSPENSION:
Swingarm with coil-over shocks

REAR BRAKE:
Drum

WEIGHT:
220 pounds

FINAL DRIVE:
Chain

OWNER:
Rich and Lynn Reed

Some of the most popular uses for the Cub were enduro, trials, and scrambles racing—its light weight and broad power range making it ideal for these off-road events. Triumph produced several models geared directly toward these applications. Tiger Cub's tall cylinder is bolted to a unit-construction engine and transmission case; Triumph's twin-cylinder models of the day carried the engine and transmission in separate cases.

1965
BMW R-27

Making its debut in 1960, the BMW R-27 was largely a rerun of the previous model, the R-26. Powered by a 250-cc vertical single, this would be the last application of such a powerplant for the German company.

Though most mechanical components were carryovers, the R-27 boasted several refinements: an automatic tensioner for the cam chain; rubber mounts for the engine/gearbox assembly and exhaust system to reduce vibration; and an increased compression ratio that raised the horsepower rating to 18. As with virtually all BMWs since the beginning of time, power was transferred to the rear wheel via shaft drive.

Up front, the unusual Earles-type leading-link fork was sprung with twin coil-over shocks, as was the strange-looking but mechanically conventional rear swingarm. The model shown sports individual "swinging saddles" in lieu of the standard two-up seat, the former supposedly providing more rider and passenger comfort.

Though it grew in popularity throughout its seven-year production run, the R-27 was dropped after 1967. The company continued with models powered by twin-cylinder "boxer" engines, long a BMW trademark.

YEAR:
1965

MANUFACTURER:
BMW

MODEL:
R-27

ENGINE TYPE:
Vertical single

DISPLACEMENT:
250 cc (approx. 15 cubic inches)

VALVE TRAIN:
Overhead valves

CARBURETION:
NA

TRANSMISSION:
Four-speed, foot shift

FRONT SUSPENSION:
Leading link with coil-over shocks

FRONT BRAKE(S):
Drum

REAR SUSPENSION:
Swingarm with coil-over shocks

REAR BRAKE:
Drum

WEIGHT:
356 pounds

FINAL DRIVE:
Shaft

OWNER:
Cloyd H. Spahr

Opposite page: Both the driver's and passenger's sprung saddles hinge at their forward edge, stretching heavy coil springs mounted underneath. Note the unusual upper mounting points for the rear shocks. *Above:* Earles-type forks were used by BMW from the mid-Fifties through the Sixties, after which they were replaced with conventional telescopic forks. It was also in the late Sixties that BMW finally abandoned its philosophy of offering "any color the customer wanted, as long as it was black." Starting in 1969, a wider palette of hues became available. *Left:* Rearview mirrors were mounted to the side of the bullet-style headlight.

1965
DKW HUMMEL 155

DKW, "Das Kleine Wonder" (the little wonder), began assembling powered cycles in 1919, and in 1932 became a partner in the Auto Union conglomerate. Most of DKW's earlier units were built with engines of at least 98 ccs of displacement, but they were always two-stroke designs.

Upon the public introduction of the Hummel 155, the European motoring press dubbed it the "Tin Banana." Its appearance was a radical departure from any contemporary offerings. In addition to the swoopy, *avant-garde* body work, the Hummel set itself apart from the competition by having a three-speed gearbox. With only a 50-cc engine producing 4.2 horsepower, the 155 was able to cruise at 45 mph. This example is fitted with a conventional foot shifter, though a hand shifter was available as an option.

The art-deco styling might have been a big hit in the U.S., but the Hummel was never exported to the States. Being readily available across Europe was not enough to illicit strong demand, and it never sold in great numbers.

YEAR:
1965

MANUFACTURER:
DKW

MODEL:
Hummel 155

ENGINE TYPE:
Vertical single

DISPLACEMENT:
50 cc (approx. 3 cubic inches)

VALVE TRAIN:
Two-stroke

CARBURETION:
Bing

TRANSMISSION:
Three-speed, foot shift (hand shift optional)

FRONT SUSPENSION:
Leading link with coil-over shocks

FRONT BRAKE(S):
Drum

REAR SUSPENSION:
Swingarm with coil-over shocks

REAR BRAKE:
Drum

WEIGHT:
NA

FINAL DRIVE:
Chain

OWNER:
Jim Kersting Family Collection

Though the Hummel may look a bit whimsical to some, its art-deco styling certainly makes it stand out today. *Opposite page:* A Darth Vader face shield covers the tiny 50-cc cylinder, while the headlight nacelle redefines the term "streamlined."

1965
DUCATI 160 MONZA JUNIOR

Ducati's history is rich with racing victories at the hands of many famous riders. The name Ducati evokes images of large, high-powered machines blasting their way into victory circles around the globe.

Along with their illustrious racing heritage, Ducati has built a large number of high-performance motorcycles for the street. Since most models grew larger and more powerful with each passing year, the introduction of the little Monza Junior seemed like an odd maneuver at the time.

Basically a Monza 250 with a reduced-displacement engine, the 156-cc Monza Junior was built on a single-loop frame that used the engine as a stressed member. Weighing less than 250 pounds, it was easy to ride and even easier to slip into tight recesses of the garage. Usually starting with a single kick of the lever, the Junior was a willing partner that was claimed to get 84 mpg, making it a frugal partner as well.

YEAR:
1965

MANUFACTURER:
Ducati

MODEL:
160 Monza Junior

ENGINE TYPE:
Vertical single

DISPLACEMENT:
156 cc (approx. 10 cubic inches)

VALVE TRAIN:
Overhead cam

CARBURETION:
Dell'Orto

TRANSMISSION:
Four-speed, foot shift

FRONT SUSPENSION:
Telescopic

FRONT BRAKE(S):
Drum

REAR SUSPENSION:
Swingarm with coil-over shocks

REAR BRAKE:
Drum

WEIGHT:
238 pounds

FINAL DRIVE:
Chain

OWNER:
Jim, Jeff, and Kevin Minnis

Left: The 160 Monza Junior had one of the smallest four-stroke, overhead-cam engines around, and like other Ducatis, the cam was driven by a spiral bevel gear system rather than a chain. *Bottom left:* Like many other bikes of the period, the speedometer was mounted in the headlight housing, but the needle's direction of travel was reversed from normal practice. *Bottom right:* Despite rather modest speed potential, the 160 got a ventilated front brake just like larger Ducatis.

1965
TRIUMPH BONNEVILLE

As America's hunger for horsepower grew, Triumph felt the need to supplant its Tiger 110 with a more powerful model. Since Triumph had pure-bred racing machines streaking across the salt flats of Utah at 150 mph, it was decided to name the new bike after this famous bastian of speed. The Bonneville would be Edward Turner's last Triumph design, and arguably his best.

Introduced in 1959, the Bonneville was powered by a 650-cc twin that inhaled through a pair of Amal carburetors. It could easily top the magical 100-mph mark, that imaginary dividing line that separated the men from the boys. As might be expected, the "Bonny" received very favorable reviews, and grew into one of Triumph's most popular models.

This 1965 Bonneville was little changed from the early versions. It was only available in Pacific Blue over Silver, but customizers in Britain and the U.S. did not spare this classic from alterations.

YEAR:
1965

MANUFACTURER:
Triumph

MODEL:
Bonneville

ENGINE TYPE:
Vertical twin

DISPLACEMENT:
650 cc (approx. 40 cubic inches)

VALVE TRAIN:
Overhead valves

CARBURETION:
Amal

TRANSMISSION:
Four-speed, foot shift

FRONT SUSPENSION:
Telescopic

FRONT BRAKE(S):
Drum

REAR SUSPENSION:
Swingarm with coil-over shocks

REAR BRAKE:
Drum

WEIGHT:
363 pounds

FINAL DRIVE:
Chain

OWNER:
Bob Baumgartner

Opposite page: Concentric-finned float bowl on the carburetor was a popular accessory of the Sixties, as were the hard Buco panniers (saddle bags). In Europe, the vertical "fin" on the front fender holds a license plate. A hinged seat that allowed easy access to the service points below it was a new feature for 1965.

1966
BENELLI FIREBALL RACER

In the mid-Sixties, club racing reached out to the private motorcycle owner and gained popularity as a low-cost form of competition throughout Europe. The machinery was usually nothing more than a street bike *sans* the excess hardware. In keeping with Benelli's racing attitude, a factory race kit was made available to those interested in winning at the club events.

The production Fireball 50-cc racer was built on a frame that was part pressed and part tubular steel, but otherwise quite conventional in layout. The Benelli race kit included a cylinder head, cylinder, crankshaft, piston, carburetor, and exhaust pipe. The strength of the 50-cc Fireball engine allowed it to be used in both the production and factory race bikes.

A 135-pound motorcycle running on skinny street tires makes for an exciting ride, regardless of the track surface, and bikes equipped with the race kit components could achieve nearly 80 mph. As a result, the Fireball racer proved quite popular, and was offered by Benelli from 1962 until 1970.

YEAR:
1966

MANUFACTURER:
Benelli

MODEL:
Fireball racer

ENGINE TYPE:
Vertical single

DISPLACEMENT:
50 cc (approx. 3 cubic inches)

VALVE TRAIN:
Two-stroke

CARBURETION:
Dell'Orto

TRANSMISSION:
Four-speed, foot shift

FRONT SUSPENSION:
Telescopic

FRONT BRAKE(S):
Drum

REAR SUSPENSION:
Swingarm with coil-over shocks

REAR BRAKE:
Drum

WEIGHT:
135 pounds

FINAL DRIVE:
Chain

OWNER:
Jonathan Jacobson

Just about as spartan as a modern motorcycle can be, the Benelli Fireball weighed in at a scant 135 pounds—less than many of its riders. *Far left:* Dell'Orto smoothbore carburetor is fitted with a velocity stack in lieu of an air cleaner. *Left:* Fuel tank wears the Benelli badge and Fireball logo. *Below:* Clip-on handlebars clamp directly to the fork legs. Forks themselves are of simple design with exposed springs.

1966
BSA SPITFIRE

L ike Triumph, BSA was a British motorcycle manufacturer whose existence revolved around a line of vertical-twin models. But by the mid-Sixties, the model line was glutted with too many variations of the same equipment. For 1966, BSA reduced its offerings to six models, each with a distinctive profile.

The A65S Spitfire was positioned as a road racer for the street. To aid performance, two large-bore Amal GP carburetors were fitted, complete with velocity stacks. As it turned out, these carbs made the Spitfire difficult to start when hot, and were often replaced with Amal concentrics with round air filters. For 1967 the factory reverted back to the concentric carburetors.

The small two-gallon fuel tank seen on this example was designed for the U.S. market in response to the popularity of the Harley Sportster's "peanut" gas tank. The European Spitfire was equipped with a four-gallon tank, and a five-gallon version was available as an option in 1967.

YEAR:
1966

MANUFACTURER:
BSA

MODEL:
Spitfire

ENGINE TYPE:
Vertical twin

DISPLACEMENT:
650 cc (approx. 40 cubic inches)

VALVE TRAIN:
Overhead valves

CARBURETION:
Amal

TRANSMISSION:
Four-speed, foot shift

FRONT SUSPENSION:
Telescopic

FRONT BRAKE(S):
Drum

REAR SUSPENSION:
Swingarm with coil-over shocks

REAR BRAKE:
Drum

WEIGHT:
408 pounds

FINAL DRIVE:
Chain

OWNER:
Jim, Jeff, and Kevin Minnis

Top left: BSA's 650-cc twins were similar in specification to those offered by Triumph, but they didn't look the same. "Teardrop" side covers and one-piece rocker covers distinguish the BSA engine. *Above:* Both Triumph and BSA made use of Smiths gauges. Note that tachometer (on right) lacks a redline; a potentially engine-scattering omission.

1966
HARLEY-DAVIDSON FLHFB

In 1965, Harley-Davidson introduced an electric-start version of the big FL series, dubbing it the Electra Glide. Still powered by the Panhead engine, the big Harley was now carrying not only the additional weight of the inevitable factory- and owner-installed accessories (made more plentiful by a switch from six- to twelve-volt electrics), but also the pounds added by the new starting hardware. Though the Panhead had served well during its lengthy tenure, owners were begging for more power, and it was time for a change.

For 1966, Harley released an updated engine. By mating new aluminum "shovelhead" cylinder heads to the iron barrels, horsepower increased by five: The FLH now claimed 60, though the FL was left with only 54.

The smoother-running, more powerful Shovelhead engine was a welcome relief. Weight of the FLs had crept up to nearly 800 pounds, and the extra power was appreciated by owners. Yet despite the greater power and escalating heft, FLs were still slowed by drum brakes, front and rear; it wouldn't be until 1972 that a front disc would appear.

YEAR:
1966

MANUFACTURER:
Harley-Davidson

MODEL:
FLHFB

ENGINE TYPE:
V-twin

DISPLACEMENT:
74 cubic inches

VALVE TRAIN:
Overhead valves

CARBURETION:
Linkert

TRANSMISSION:
Four-speed, foot shift
(hand shift optional)

FRONT SUSPENSION:
Telescopic

FRONT BRAKE(S):
Drum

REAR SUSPENSION:
Swingarm with coil-over shocks

REAR BRAKE:
Drum

WEIGHT:
764 pounds

FINAL DRIVE:
Chain

OWNER:
John Archacki

Windshield, dual spotlights, and a backrest for the Buddy seat were all popular accessories for Harley's Big Twin, as were the numerous chrome trim pieces. The new Shovelhead engine *(below right)* had distinctly different valve covers than the Panhead engine that preceded it, and produced about five more horsepower.

119

1966
MOTOBI IMPERIALE SPORT

The roots of the Motobi can be readily traced back to 1911 when Benelli began building its motorcycles in Pesaro, Italy. There were six Benelli brothers who founded the company, but around 1950, Giuseppe set off to build his own line of motorcycles at another location in Pesaro.

Calling his company Motobi, Giuseppe's first model was powered by a 98-cc single that he designed himself, and he soon set out to conquer the racetracks of Italy. For a number of years, Motobi did just that, taking the Italian F3 championship every year between 1959 and 1972.

As the list of racing victories grew, so did the displacement of Motobi's street machines. The 125-cc model shown was joined by 175-, 200-, and 250-cc versions, all of them virtually identical in outward appearance.

Strangely enough, the other Benelli brothers brought Giuseppe back into the fold when they purchased Motobi in the late Seventies. Thereafter, the Motobi name would continue to be used on the top-of-the-line Benellis for many years to come.

YEAR:
1966

MANUFACTURER:
Motobi

MODEL:
Imperiale Sport

ENGINE TYPE:
Horizontal single

DISPLACEMENT:
125 cc (approx. 7.6 cubic inches)

VALVE TRAIN:
Overhead valves

CARBURETION:
Dell'Orto

TRANSMISSION:
Five-speed, foot shift

FRONT SUSPENSION:
Telescopic

FRONT BRAKE(S):
Drum

REAR SUSPENSION:
Swingarm with coil-over shocks

REAR BRAKE:
Drum

WEIGHT:
190 pounds

FINAL DRIVE:
Chain

OWNER:
Jonathan Jacobson

Far left: Dell'Orto carb was positioned at a severe angle to feed the horizontal cylinder; note separate vertically mounted float bowl. Engine itself was very compact, and looked similar to the Italian-built horizontal single offered by Harley-Davidson during the same period. *Left:* Short clip-on handlebars clamped directly to the fork legs; note severe inboard positioning of brake lever.

1967
HARLEY-DAVIDSON XLH

After the initial euphoria surrounding the XL's introduction 10 years earlier, Harley-Davidson started to build Sportsters aimed at filling more specific niches in the market. To enhance their appeal for 1967, Sportsters were offered with the electric starting system introduced on the big FL series two years earlier. Two versions of the XL were offered: the XLCH kept its kick starter and was aimed at the performance market, while the electric-start XLH was polished up and pushed as its well-dressed counterpart.

A typical XLCH would usually be found with a sprung solo saddle that enhanced its racebike image. The XLH, however, was often seen with a cushy two-place seat complete with matching padded backrest. Adding to the XLH's flair was an aluminum headlight nacelle and enclosed rear shocks aimed at giving a clean, contemporary look. The two-tone, black-and-white paint scheme was carried into the tank badges and the seat cover.

Though both versions carried an 883-cc V-twin engine, the XLCH outsold the XLH; apparently, the Sportster was still considered more of a performance machine than a styling statement. But that would soon change.

YEAR:
1967

MANUFACTURER:
Harley-Davidson

MODEL:
XLH

ENGINE TYPE:
V-twin

DISPLACEMENT:
883 cc (approx. 54 cubic inches)

VALVE TRAIN:
Overhead valves

CARBURETION:
NA

TRANSMISSION:
Four-speed, foot shift

FRONT SUSPENSION:
Telescopic

FRONT BRAKE(S):
Drum

REAR SUSPENSION:
Swingarm with coil-over shocks

REAR BRAKE:
Drum

WEIGHT:
NA

FINAL DRIVE:
Chain

OWNER:
Al and Pat Doerman

Opposite page: XLH was fitted with both an electric starter—new for '67—and a kick starter; some later models had only one or the other. *Above:* Large, polished headlight nacelle was a precursor to the "eyebrow" nacelle that later became a Sportster trademark, and was also used on some custom versions of Harley's big FL series. *Left:* Chrome bezel surrounded the speedometer and tach, another custom touch on the XLH.

1967
TRIUMPH T100C

Throughout the Fifties and Sixties, Triumph sold a complete line of small and mid-size motorcycles aimed at intermediate riders. One of the most popular was the Tiger 100, which was introduced in 1960 as the T100A. A vertical twin of 500-cc displacement, it wore two-tone paint and "bathtub" tank badges.

In 1966, the Tiger received a thorough makeover. A new frame was complimented with better forks that improved handling and stability. Two-tone paint continued, but tank badges were changed to a new "eyebrow" style.

Offered alongside the T100A touring model was the T100C, an on/off road bike that sported a smaller fuel tank and headlight, along with high-mounted twin exhaust pipes. A skidplate was added to protect the underside of the engine during off-road excursions, and an alternator replaced the old Energy Transfer electric system. U.S. versions received alloy fenders in place of the steel units found on their European counterparts.

T100 models continued to be popular right into the Seventies, when in 1973 the T100C was reborn as the TR5T Trophy Trail.

YEAR:
1967

MANUFACTURER:
Triumph

MODEL:
T100C

ENGINE TYPE:
Vertical twin

DISPLACEMENT:
500 cc (approx. 30 cubic inches)

VALVE TRAIN:
Overhead valves

CARBURETION:
Amal

TRANSMISSION:
Four-speed, foot shift

FRONT SUSPENSION:
Telescopic

FRONT BRAKE(S):
Drum

REAR SUSPENSION:
Swingarm with coil-over shocks

REAR BRAKE:
Drum

WEIGHT:
335 pounds

FINAL DRIVE:
Chain

OWNER:
George Pilacek

Far Left: Tiger's 500-cc twin looked very similar to Triumph's 650-cc engine, though the latter had larger cooling fins on the head and added fins on the rocker covers. *Left:* "Eyebrow" tank badges were adopted in 1966. Tiger engine was fed by a single Amal carburetor; the sportier 500-cc Daytona, introduced in '67, carried dual carbs.

1968
HARLEY-DAVIDSON CR250

In 1961, Harley-Davidson joined with Italian partner Aermacchi to produce the Sprint, a 250-cc four-stroke single that was intended as an intermediate step for those intimidated by the size and price of Harley's larger V-twins. With adequate power and relatively light weight, it was a joy around town and proved quite popular.

Developed as a racing permutation of the Sprint, the CR250 was built in several variations through the years, but the flat-trackers ended up drawing the most attention. During the Sixties, several national championships were won by steel-toed riders mounted on Harley iron. It wasn't until the two-stroke machines from Japan made their presence known that the CR250 lost its competitive edge.

This CR250 is set up much like the winning race bikes of the Sixties. The engine has been internally modified and sports a compression ratio of 12:1. The Dell'Orto carburetor supplied by the factory has been replaced by a modern Mikuni. With these modifications, a total of 35 horsepower is on tap at 10,000 rpm. Also, the Harley-Davidson forks have been upgraded to Ceriani's from Italy, and the rear end is devoid of suspension.

No more than 50 CR250's were built in any year between 1966 and 1970, making them a favorite choice of vintage race-bike collectors.

YEAR:
1968

MANUFACTURER:
Harley-Davidson

MODEL:
CR250

ENGINE TYPE:
Horizontal single

DISPLACEMENT:
251 cc (approx. 15 cubic inches)

VALVE TRAIN:
Double overhead cams

CARBURETION:
Mikuni

TRANSMISSION:
Five-speed, foot shift

FRONT SUSPENSION:
Telescopic

FRONT BRAKE(S):
None

REAR SUSPENSION:
Rigid

REAR BRAKE:
None

WEIGHT:
215 pounds

FINAL DRIVE:
Chain

OWNER:
Dave Kiesow

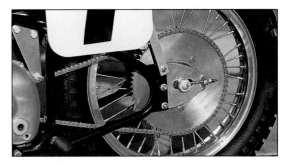

Left: CR250 horizontal single used a twin-cam head and lofty 12:1 compression to produce 35 horsepower from 251 ccs—better than two horsepower per cubic inch. *Above:* A solid rear subframe replaced the standard model's swingarm suspension. Being a flattracker, brakes were considered superfluous.

1968
HARLEY-DAVIDSON XLCH

The XL Sportster bowed in 1957 and was an overnight success. Faster and more powerful than its K Model predecessor, it allowed Harley-Davidson to once again send the motorcycle world into a frenzy.

Almost before the first batch of XLs hit the road, however, people wanted even more. The XLCH was the result of combining two earlier versions of the Sportster, the XLC and the XLH. This cross-breeding took place in 1962, and the result was often referred to as the "competition hot" model. With the advent of electric starting in 1967, the XLH gained that convenience, while the XLCH was equipped only with a kick starter due to its niche in the competition segment of the market.

An important event in Harley's history took place in 1969. After more than 65 years under family ownership, Harley-Davidson was purchased by sporting-goods manufacturer AMF, and Harley's '69 models carried an AMF logo—as they would for the next dozen years.

YEAR:
1968

MANUFACTURER:
Harley-Davidson

MODEL:
XLCH

ENGINE TYPE:
V-twin

DISPLACEMENT:
883 cc (approx. 54 cubic inches)

VALVE TRAIN:
Overhead valves

CARBURETION:
NA

TRANSMISSION:
Four-speed, foot shift

FRONT SUSPENSION:
Telescopic

FRONT BRAKE(S):
Drum

REAR SUSPENSION:
Swingarm with coil-over shocks

REAR BRAKE:
Drum

WEIGHT:
NA

FINAL DRIVE:
Chain

OWNER:
Ted Moran

Though the "luxury oriented" XLH boasted electric starting in 1968, the XLCH had only a kick starter. That didn't seem to hurt the latter's popularity, however, as it accounted for nearly 20 percent of Harley's sales that year. The XLCH shown here is a good example of a period unit. The solo seat is sprung into the vertical frame tube, much like the old "Full-Floeting" saddle on very early Harleys. The luggage rack and "Hi-Fi Blue" paint with black crinkle inset on top of the tank were other popular features of the time.

1968
KREIDLER FLORETT RS

Kreidler's business was mopeds, and had been since the company opened its doors in 1951. Regardless of model, they were always powered by 50-cc two-strokes. Kreidlers were available only in their home country of Germany until the early Sixties, after which distribution spread across Europe, and a few found their way to the U.S.

Needless to say, the Florett RS pictured is no moped. It is a factory-built racing machine built on a tubular frame (the mopeds had stamped-steel frames), powered by a 50-cc racing engine. By converting the standard piston port intake to a disc valve, horsepower rose from 15 to 18—in either case, an impressive output for a 50-cc engine.

The little Kreidler was introduced to the racetracks in 1961, and though top speed hovered near 100 mph, it was another 10 years before the Florett won its first title. Five more followed, but the company's financial condition worsened, and the factory was closed in 1982 after an unsuccessful change of ownership the previous year.

YEAR:
1968

MANUFACTURER:
Kreidler

MODEL:
Florett RS

ENGINE TYPE:
Horizontal single

DISPLACEMENT:
50 cc (approx. 3 cubic inches)

VALVE TRAIN:
Two-stroke

CARBURETION:
Bing

TRANSMISSION:
Five-speed, foot shift

FRONT SUSPENSION:
Telescopic

FRONT BRAKE(S):
Drum

REAR SUSPENSION:
Swingarm with coil-over shocks

REAR BRAKE:
Drum

WEIGHT:
130 pounds

FINAL DRIVE:
Chain

OWNER:
Erich Bley

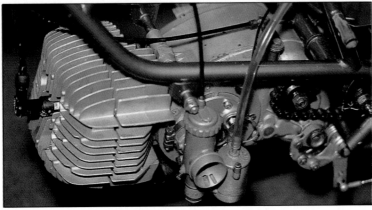

Above: Being a racing bike, the Florett's pilot was afforded little luxury; note the tiny, thinly padded seat. Clip-on handlebars, which mounted directly to the fork tubes, forced the rider into a very crouched position to minimize wind resistance. Note the gold-colored brake hubs, a classy touch for such a purpose-built bike. *Left:* Racing versions of the 50-cc two-stroke engine received a disc valve in place of the normal piston-port intake.

1969
BSA FIREBIRD SCRAMBLER

To support the claim that its 1969 model line was "the bold way to make time," BSA offered seven different models that included two singles, four twins, and a three-cylinder bike, the Rocket 3. After 60-plus years of building motorcycles, BSA was offering a lot of contemporary hardware to the crowded British market.

The A65FS, or Firebird Scrambler, was filling the need for a versatile two-wheeled vehicle. With an eight-inch ground clearance, lower-engine skid plate, and waist-high dual exhausts, the Scrambler was dressed for both on- and off-road action. Furthermore, its 650-cc engine ran with 9:1 compression for additional horsepower.

The Firebird Scrambler was only available in red, and featured rubber-mounted instruments for quick assessment of its vital signs. Production only continued into 1971, when single-purpose machines became more prevalent.

YEAR:
1969

MANUFACTURER:
BSA

MODEL:
Firebird Scrambler

ENGINE TYPE:
Vertical twin

DISPLACEMENT:
650 cc (approx. 40 cubic inches)

VALVE TRAIN:
Overhead valves

CARBURETION:
NA

TRANSMISSION:
Four-speed, foot shift

FRONT SUSPENSION:
Telescopic

FRONT BRAKE(S):
Drum

REAR SUSPENSION:
Swingarm with coil-over shocks

REAR BRAKE:
Drum

WEIGHT:
421 pounds

FINAL DRIVE:
Chain

OWNER:
Matt Jonas

Top Left: For 1969, the Firebird Scrambler gained a ventilated eight-inch twin-leading-shoe front brake. *Top right:* BSA logo changed several times over the company's history, and sometimes varied on different models built the same year. *Above:* Firebird Scrambler featured high-mounted exhaust pipes with an exhaust equalizer that increased horsepower. A chromed guard protected the rider's leg from the heat.

1969
BSA Rocket 3

In 1968, BSA augmented its lineup of traditional singles and twins with the imposing three-cylinder Rocket 3. Nearly a clone of the Triumph Trident, the Rocket 3 was powered by an alloy 750-cc engine producing 58 horsepower that could propel the bike to near 120 mph. Later models would have even more power and higher top speeds. In 1971, a Rocket 3 was ridden to victory at the Daytona 200; however, it would prove to be a farewell appearance.

The Rocket 3's contemporary styling and ample power were not enough to fend off the stampede of new large-displacement motorcycles coming out of Japan. BSA ceased production of its own models by 1973, after which it was rolled into the Norton-Villiers-Triumph group.

YEAR:
1969

MANUFACTURER:
BSA

MODEL:
Rocket 3

ENGINE TYPE:
Inline three

DISPLACEMENT:
750 cc (approx. 45 cubic inches)

VALVE TRAIN:
Overhead valves

CARBURETION:
Amal

TRANSMISSION:
Four-speed, foot shift

FRONT SUSPENSION:
Telescopic

FRONT BRAKE(S):
Drum

REAR SUSPENSION:
Swingarm with coil-over shocks

REAR BRAKE:
Drum

WEIGHT:
495 pounds

FINAL DRIVE:
Chain

OWNER:
Ben Frame

When introduced, BSA's Rocket 3 was one of the more powerful bikes around, but it would soon be overshadowed by Honda's 750 Four. The Rocket 3 was instantly recognizable by its "ray gun" mufflers with their trio of protruding pipes. *Above:* Note the "pie tin" covers for the front drum brake. *Left:* Traditional Smiths gauges provided a clean look from the rider's seat. Later models, with a bit more power and taller gearing, could pull the speedometer needle to 130.

1969
HONDA DREAM 305

Soichiro Honda's first effort, the 98-cc two-stroke Model D of 1947, was considered quite rough when compared to its competition. Since then, however, the company that bears his name has undergone some radical changes.

After years of development and growth, Honda found itself flirting with bankruptcy in 1953. But it managed to hang on, and in 1958, the C100 Super Cub was introduced. Powered by a 50-cc four-stroke single, it was an instant hit. The Cub's light weight and step-through design appealed to a large audience, and by 1960, Honda was shipping more than 169,000 units per year to 50 countries around the globe.

The Dream 305 followed in its footsteps, and likewise enjoyed robust sales. Like its forbearer, it was light and easy to handle; but with its 305-cc twin-cylinder engine, it was far more powerful, with a top speed of nearly 100 mph.

Amazingly, its production run would last 10 years. By the late Sixties, consumer interest was moving towards larger, more powerful motorcycles, and Honda replaced the Dream with larger twins and the formidable 750 Four.

YEAR:
1969

MANUFACTURER:
Honda

MODEL:
Dream 305

ENGINE TYPE:
Vertical twin

DISPLACEMENT:
305 cc (approx. 19 cubic inches)

VALVE TRAIN:
Overhead cams

CARBURETION:
Keihin

TRANSMISSION:
Four-speed, foot shift

FRONT SUSPENSION:
Leading link with enclosed coil-over shocks

FRONT BRAKE(S):
Drum

REAR SUSPENSION:
Swingarm with coil-over shocks

REAR BRAKE:
Drum

WEIGHT:
NA

FINAL DRIVE:
Chain

OWNER:
Bill Yoakum

The Dream could be dressed up with a dizzying array of saddlebags, luggage racks, and windshields to increase its usefulness and individualize its personality. *Left:* Gear-shift lever had both toe and heel pads for easy shifting. *Bottom Left:* Stamped-steel mufflers showed a prominent seam along the edges. *Below:* Fuel tank boasted chrome side plates and rubber knee pads.

1969
HONDA CB750

In June of 1968, Honda dropped the gauntlet that would forever change the world of motorcycling. The CB750 Four offered a combination of hardware never before seen on a single machine.

It wasn't just the four-cylinder engine; though most competitors were twins, fours had been offered by several manufacturers in the past. No, it was the fact that four-cylinder power and smoothness were joined by a five-speed gearbox, electric starter, and a front disc brake—the first ever on a street machine—all at a reasonable price.

By 1970, Dick Mann piloted a race-prepped CB750 into the winner's circle at Daytona, and the world of aftermarket hop-up equipment came alive. The CB750 is also credited with casting the mold for what would later be called the "Universal Japanese Motorcycle," a breed of machines that would bring the bikes of Europe to their collective knees.

YEAR:
1969

MANUFACTURER:
Honda

MODEL:
CB750

ENGINE TYPE:
Inline four

DISPLACEMENT:
750 cc (approx. 45 cubic inches)

VALVE TRAIN:
Overhead cam

CARBURETION:
Keihin

TRANSMISSION:
Five-speed, foot shift

FRONT SUSPENSION:
Telescopic

FRONT BRAKE(S):
Disc

REAR SUSPENSION:
Swingarm with coil-over shocks

REAR BRAKE:
Drum

WEIGHT:
498 pounds

FINAL DRIVE:
Chain

OWNER:
Ray Landy

The first CB750s were produced with sand-cast cases that had a rough finish; later models had smoother castings. Those early models, such as the bike pictured, also had an additional horsepower on tap, and because of their rarity, have become the most valuable to collectors. *Left:* Early CB750s had a separate oil tank, which was hidden beneath the side cover along with the air cleaner.

1970
BSA LIGHTNING

BSA began building motorcycles just after the turn of the century, and prospered through economic downturns and two world wars. The company took controlling interest of Triumph in 1951 and recorded record profits heading into the Sixties. But by the time the 1970 models hit showroom floors, BSA was struggling to keep its head above water.

The culprits, of course, were the cheaper—and often faster—Japanese motorcycles such as the Honda 750 Four, Yamaha 650 twin, and various Kawasaki and Suzuki large-displacement two-strokes.

Due to its proven track record, the 650-cc vertical twin used in the Lightning was also the powerplant of choice for several other BSA models. But because funds were beginning to dry up, the company made few product changes in 1970. Among those few changes were better brakes for the Lightning, which now sported an eight-inch drum with twin leading shoes up front, and a seven-inch drum in back.

BSA didn't survive long afterward, however, the competition from Japan proving to be too much for the beleaguered company. Triumph continued to scrape along for another decade or so, until it too finally succumbed to the Japanese onslaught.

YEAR:
1970

MANUFACTURER:
BSA

MODEL:
Lightning

ENGINE TYPE:
Vertical twin

DISPLACEMENT:
650 cc (approx. 40 cubic inches)

VALVE TRAIN:
Overhead valves

CARBURETION:
Amal

TRANSMISSION:
Five-speed, foot shift

FRONT SUSPENSION:
Telescopic

FRONT BRAKE(S):
Drum

REAR SUSPENSION:
Swingarm with coil-over shocks

REAR BRAKE:
Drum

WEIGHT:
NA

FINAL DRIVE:
Chain

OWNER:
Jim Wetzel

Above: For 1970, the Lighting gained an eight-inch, twin-leading-shoe front brake with a racing-type air scoop on the right side. Also new was the passenger grab rail that surrounded the rear section of the seat *(opposite page)*. This would be the last of BSA's twins to have an oil tank beneath the seat; starting in 1971, the oil was carried in the "backbone" frame tube.

1970
NORTON COMMANDO 750S

In its attempt to recapture some of the customers escaping to other machines, Norton created the Commando for 1968. By combining a strong frame, vertical-twin engine, and rubber mounting points, the Isolastic System was born. By reducing vibration, it was hoped that this model could successfully battle the newcomers from Japan.

Aside from the Isolastic System, much of the Commando's hardware was common to other Norton models. At the front end, Roadholder forks were lengthened and held eight-inch, twin-leading-shoe brakes. Out back, the Girling shocks could be adjusted to one of three settings to optimize comfort and handling. The time-tested vertical-twin engine featured cylinder heads, push rods, and connecting rods made of aluminum.

The Commando appeared in several configurations during its lifetime, and the "S" model first arrived in 1969. Its distinctive high exhaust pipes with heat shields set the S apart from other Commandos. More importantly, the S stood for Sport, and magazine reviews raved about the new levels of performance.

The dual seat was upholstered with a tuck-and-roll cover, and the 2.7-gallon fuel tank looked sleek and sporty, but it didn't offer much range. Despite its 125-mph capabilities, the S model slipped into oblivion during the 1970 model year, though the Commando line itself continued on into the mid-Seventies.

YEAR:
1970

MANUFACTURER:
Norton

MODEL:
Commando 750S

ENGINE TYPE:
Vertical twin

DISPLACEMENT:
745 cc (approx. 45 cubic inches)

VALVE TRAIN:
Overhead valves

CARBURETION:
Amal

TRANSMISSION:
Four-speed, foot shift

FRONT SUSPENSION:
Telescopic

FRONT BRAKE(S):
Drum

REAR SUSPENSION:
Swingarm with coil-over shocks

REAR BRAKE:
Drum

WEIGHT:
415 pounds

FINAL DRIVE:
Chain

OWNER:
Matt Jonas

The Commando 750S differed from its siblings in having high-mounted exhaust pipes. Normally, these would be found on "Scramblers," which were on/off-road versions of regular street bikes. *Above:* Note large, chrome automotive-style air cleaner.

1970
TRIUMPH DAYTONA

In the spring of 1966, a Triumph in racing trim was ridden to victory at the world-famous Daytona Speedway. Not only was rider Buddy Elmore credited with the win, he was also indirectly responsible for the creation of a new sporting machine.

Triumph rolled out the new Daytona model the following year. Though it displaced only 500 ccs, it was packed with performance parts. A redesigned combustion chamber resulted in a compression ratio of 9:1, and each cylinder was fed through its own Amal concentric carburetor. A new frame design increased steering head rake for crisper handling, and also allowed the seat height to be reduced in response to the common complaint of an overly tall saddle. In 1970, a chrome grab rail was added to the rear of the two-person seat.

Early Daytonas were stopped with an eight-inch drum brake up front and a seven-inch drum in the rear. The front brake would later be changed to a seven-inch drum with twin leading shoes inside.

Since the Daytona was aimed at U.S. distribution, color schemes were chosen that would reflect trends seen in the American automotive market. One of the more interesting combinations is seen on this 1970 model: Jacaranda Purple with silver accents.

YEAR:
1970

MANUFACTURER:
Triumph

MODEL:
Daytona

ENGINE TYPE:
Vertical twin

DISPLACEMENT:
500 cc (approx. 30 cubic inches)

VALVE TRAIN:
Overhead valves

CARBURETION:
Amal

TRANSMISSION:
Four-speed, foot shift

FRONT SUSPENSION:
Telescopic

FRONT BRAKE(S):
Drum

REAR SUSPENSION:
Swingarm with coil-over shocks

REAR BRAKE:
Drum

WEIGHT:
NA

FINAL DRIVE:
Chain

OWNER:
Marty Feldkamp

A "high performance" 500-cc bike might seem an odd addition to the Triumph line when the company also offered 650-cc machines. But the lighter, cheaper Daytona didn't give up much in the performance department to its big brothers and sold fairly well—partly because it differed little in appearance except for color scheme.

1970
TRIUMPH TIGER 650

Throughout the 1960s, England found its economy slipping into a sea of red ink. Many large companies were closing their doors and unemployment was rampant. As a method of keeping some of these firms afloat, the government offered infusions of cash as long as the firm would also take on engineers from the bloated military pool. Although the capital was a welcome relief, engineers that were hired by various motorcycle manufacturers thought like engineers rather than motorcycle enthusiasts, and many of the changes that came about were questionable at best.

Triumph had offered a wide variety of machines throughout its history, but vertical twins, starting with the 500-cc Speed Twin of 1937, soon became the most popular. By the Fifties, the engine had grown to 650 ccs as found in the Thunderbird, and later the Bonneville and Tiger models.

Both the Bonneville and Tiger were fitted with the same basic engine, but the latter had only one carburetor, trading horsepower for easier starting and better fuel economy. As a result, the Tiger was slower than the Bonneville, but was considered to be a better all-around choice for many riders.

Bonneville and Tiger grew to 750 ccs for the 1973 model year, but their days were numbered; the Japanese, with their more advanced machines, were about to take over.

YEAR:
1970

MANUFACTURER:
Triumph

MODEL:
Tiger

ENGINE TYPE:
Vertical twin

DISPLACEMENT:
650 cc (approx. 40 cubic inches)

VALVE TRAIN:
Overhead valves

CARBURETION:
Amal

TRANSMISSION:
Five-speed, foot shift

FRONT SUSPENSION:
Telescopic

FRONT BRAKE(S):
Drum

REAR SUSPENSION:
Swingarm with coil-over shocks

REAR BRAKE:
Drum

WEIGHT:
430 pounds

FINAL DRIVE:
Chain

OWNER:
Dick Cogswell

Tiger was the single-carb stablemate of the more famous Bonneville. Though the latter was faster, its Amal carburetors were renowned for going out of sync, which made the engine run poorly. With its lone carburetor, the Tiger was easier to keep tuned. Like the Bonneville, it carried a ventilated front drum brake *(left)* and Smiths gauges *(far left)*.

1970
TRACKMASTER

With the widespread popularity of flat-track racing in the Sixties, a variety of custom frame builders sprang up on the West coast. Champion, Redline, and several others built tubular frames that would accept a variety of engines, but Trackmaster proved to be one of the most popular. Intended for flat-track use only, a Trackmaster frame was delivered with nickel plating covering every inch of the tubing.

Triumph engines had long been used in various racing applications, and they often found their way into these custom-framed flat-trackers. Oftentimes, the stock 650-cc engine was fitted with a stroker crank or large-bore pistons, usually resulting in a displacement of about 750 ccs, though sometimes even more.

After stints on the racing circuits, many riders converted their flat-trackers into street machines by adding the required lighting at both ends. Of course, brakes were another worthwhile addition (flat-trackers having no need for them), with the example shown being fitted with dual discs up front and a single rotor out back.

The sturdy construction of the Trackmaster chassis is evidenced by the reinforcing gussets at the steering head. Bolted to this steering head is a substantial Ceriani racing fork and a tiny plastic fender. A racing component that hasn't been replaced is the sinister-looking black exhaust system—something that isn't likely to be appreciated in a residential neighborhood.

YEAR:
1970

MANUFACTURER:
Trackmaster

MODEL:
—

ENGINE TYPE:
Vertical twin

DISPLACEMENT:
750 cc (approx. 45 cubic inches)

VALVE TRAIN:
Overhead valves

CARBURETION:
NA

TRANSMISSION:
Four-speed, foot shift

FRONT SUSPENSION:
Telescopic

FRONT BRAKE(S):
Dual discs

REAR SUSPENSION:
Swingarm with coil-over shocks

REAR BRAKE:
Disc

WEIGHT:
NA

FINAL DRIVE:
Chain

OWNER:
Dick Cogswell

Transforming a flat-track racer into a street bike was no easy—or cheap—trick. The example shown had to have a lighting system added, as well as brakes. Whoever modified this machine didn't scrimp on the latter; this triple-disc setup provides plenty of stopping power. The locals, however, no doubt wished that a little more money had been spent on proper mufflers.

1971
HARLEY-DAVIDSON FX SUPERGLIDE

In an effort to compete head-on with the aftermarket suppliers, Harley-Davidson ushered in its first "factory custom" for the 1971 model year. By combining pieces from two popular models, the "Big Twin" FL and the XL Sportster, the company hoped to provide buyers with a new breed of Harley.

Stripped of its electric starter, the FX could be fitted with a smaller battery and battery box. The forks and front wheel were taken from the XL's parts bin, as was a smaller-diameter headlight and trademark headlight cover. The frame, 74-cubic-inch Shovelhead engine, and rear suspension originated from the FL. The dual tanks were from the FLH. A fiberglass tail section was styled after a similar piece used on the previous year's Sportster, and all the bodywork was covered with a special Sparkling America paint scheme.

New and exciting as it was, the market failed to respond to the first Superglide, and only 4700 found buyers. By comparison, over 10,000 Sportsters were sold in the same year.

The Superglide returned for 1972, but some of its pieces did not. The tail section disappeared, replaced by a traditional, steel fender assembly. In this form, the Superglide met with greater success, and factory customs would eventually become Harley-Davidson's stock in trade.

YEAR:
1971

MANUFACTURER:
Harley-Davidson

MODEL:
FX Superglide

ENGINE TYPE:
V-twin

DISPLACEMENT:
74 cubic inches

VALVE TRAIN:
Overhead valves

CARBURETION:
Bendix

TRANSMISSION:
Four-speed, foot shift

FRONT SUSPENSION:
Telescopic

FRONT BRAKE(S):
Drum

REAR SUSPENSION:
Swingarm with coil-over shocks

REAR BRAKE:
Drum

WEIGHT:
560 pounds

FINAL DRIVE:
Chain

OWNER:
Jim Kersting Family Collection

Although Harley's original factory custom didn't go over very well, many who turned it down no doubt regret their decision today. "Boat tail" rear fender was styled after the one that debuted on the 1970 Sportster, but while the two looked similar, they were not interchangeable. Sportster forks, with their trademark "eyebrow" casting over the headlight and fork brace below it, lent the big Superglide a lighter, dragster-like look.

1971
NORTON COMMANDO FASTBACK LR

With Norton's competition machines cleaning up in road-racing events during the early Sixties, the company's production bikes were expected to exhibit similar levels of performance. But it wasn't until the 1968 introduction of the Commando series that Norton's winning reputation was transferred to the street.

The Commando, or 20M3, was an immediate success with both the media and the buying public. One magazine named it "Machine of the Year" not only in 1968, but also in '69, '70, and '71.

A new isolastic engine-mounting system that reduced vibration was a big contributor to the Commando's new-found popularity. Up front, Commandos carried "Roadholder" forks and an eight-inch twin-leading-shoe drum brake.

Powered by a 745-cc Atlas engine, the Commando was a potent performer. It was so well sorted out by this time that very few mechanical alterations were made to the engine, gearbox, or suspension for several years.

Changes that were made fell into the category of cosmetics. Norton offered several variations of the Commando, the Fastback LR (Long Range) model shown being named for its slick tailpiece and large-capacity fuel tank. Available in either red or green, production was very limited: Between 1971 and 1973, only about 400 of these classic motorcycles were built.

YEAR:
1971

MANUFACTURER:
Norton

MODEL:
Commando Fastback LR

ENGINE TYPE:
Vertical twin

DISPLACEMENT:
745 cc (approx. 45 cubic inches)

VALVE TRAIN:
Overhead valves

CARBURETION:
Amal

TRANSMISSION:
Four-speed, foot shift

FRONT SUSPENSION:
Telescopic

FRONT BRAKE(S):
Drum

REAR SUSPENSION:
Swingarm with coil-over shocks

REAR BRAKE:
Drum

WEIGHT:
410 pounds

FINAL DRIVE:
Chain

OWNER:
Bob Marin

Norton's Commando was probably the quickest production bike money could buy—for about one year. Soon after its 1968 debut, Honda brought out the powerful CB750 Four and Kawasaki released its ferocious Mach III 500-cc two-stroke triple. Still, the Commando, with its antiquated but well-designed overhead-valve twin *(far left)* remained in the running. Though later 850-cc versions would adopt a modern front disc, 750-cc models used a ventilated drum brake *(left)*.

1973
DUNSTALL NORTON 850 MK 3

In 1967, Paul Dunstall began tweaking, tuning, and streamlining factory-spec motorcycles to increase their performance. By 1973, there were seven different models in his catalog, one of which was the Dunstall Norton 850 shown on these pages.

Starting with a Norton 850 Commando, Dunstall trimmed the curb weight by substituting lightweight plastic and fiberglass body parts for the stock steel components. A bullet-shaped fairing was added to the front to cut wind resistance at high speeds, and a tailpiece was added to cut drag.

Of course, not all modifications were cosmetic. Inside Norton's famed vertical twin engine, the stock pistons gave way to high-performance slugs that raised the compression ratio to 9.5:1. The special Dunstall "Power Exhaust" header system joined the two headpipes together beneath the frame, and then split them again before they flowed into separate megaphone mufflers.

U.S.-bound Mk 3s wore larger fairings than were fitted to European Mk 4 versions, and were also equipped with turn signals in accordance with federal regulations. Behind the fairing sat a tidy instrument cluster above narrow clip-on handlebars, the latter of which severely limited the bike's turning radius. But then, the Dunstall Norton was not designed with low-speed maneuvers in mind.

YEAR:
1973

MANUFACTURER:
Dunstall Norton

MODEL:
850 Mk 3

ENGINE TYPE:
Vertical twin

DISPLACEMENT:
850 cc (approx. 52 cubic inches)

VALVE TRAIN:
Overhead valves

CARBURETION:
Amal

TRANSMISSION:
Four-speed, foot shift

FRONT SUSPENSION:
Telescopic

FRONT BRAKE(S):
Disc

REAR SUSPENSION:
Swingarm with coil-over shocks

REAR BRAKE:
Drum

WEIGHT:
440 pounds

FINAL DRIVE:
Chain

OWNER:
Matt Jonas

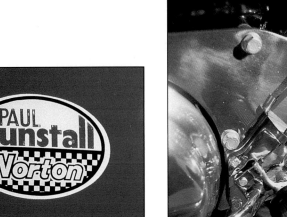

When Paul Dunstall massaged a bike, it gained more than just sporty-looking bodywork. In this case, the engine was elevated to a higher state of tune, the stock steel rims were replaced with lightweight aluminum wheels that decreased unsprung weight, and the tires were upgraded to Dunlop TT100s. *Left:* Note the custom-made "signatured" mounting plate for the rear-set footpegs.

1973
KAWASAKI Z-1

After Honda debuted the CB750 in 1969, other Japanese manufacturers scrambled to best the effort. One of the most notable outcomes of this mad scramble was Kawasaki's Z-1.

Introduced in 1973, the Z-1 boasted a 903-cc double-overhead-cam inline four that significantly upped the performance ante. That engine soon became the benchmark other companies would aim to beat, and it proved to be a bulletproof design that continues to be a dominant force in racing circles to this day.

In contrast to the strong-running powerplant, the chassis of the Z-1 was notoriously unstable. Several aftermarket manufacturers quickly devised more competent frame designs that could be filled with Z-1 power.

No color options were offered for the U.S. market, all Z-1s being painted brown with orange accents. Not considered a particularly appealing combination at the time, many early Z-1s received custom paint treatments very early in their careers.

YEAR:
1973

MANUFACTURER:
Kawasaki

MODEL:
Z-1

ENGINE TYPE:
Inline four

DISPLACEMENT:
903 cc (approx. 55 cubic inches)

VALVE TRAIN:
Double overhead cams

CARBURETION:
Mikuni

TRANSMISSION:
Five-speed, foot shift

FRONT SUSPENSION:
Telescopic

FRONT BRAKE(S):
Disc

REAR SUSPENSION:
Swingarm with coil-over shocks

REAR BRAKE:
Drum

WEIGHT:
506 pounds

FINAL DRIVE:
Chain

OWNER:
Al Steier

Though following the same formula as Honda's 750 Four, the Z-1 upped the Superbike ante when it was introduced in 1973. It's rare to find an early Z-1 wearing its original paint and rarer still to find one with its stock exhaust system; the factory-installed four-into-one exhaust worked well, but was rather thin-walled and usually soon replaced with an aftermarket header.

1973
MOTO GUZZI 850 ELDORADO

The Moto Guzzi 850 Eldorado is not a small motorcycle, nor was it designed to be. Weighing in at nearly 600 pounds with a full load of fuel, the Eldorado sounds ponderous, and the large fuel tank and hunkered-down profile do nothing to trim its appearance. But as large as it may appear, the Eldorado actually has a shorter wheelbase than a Honda CB750.

With a displacement increase of 100 ccs over the previous model, the 850 Eldorado is designed to devour highway miles at high speed with little strain. The long, flat saddle is wide enough to support nearly any rider and passenger with ease, and the handlebars rise up to greet the rider's hands in their natural extension. Along with an electric tachometer and mechanical speedometer are a bank of four indicator lights.

Our featured Eldorado is equipped with a Monaco sidecar, the lines of which seem to complement the bike's heavy curves, right down to the chrome trim rail on the nose. The seating area of the Monaco would be right at home in your living room, allowing a lucky passenger to soak up the miles in great comfort.

YEAR:
1973

MANUFACTURER:
Moto Guzzi

MODEL:
850 Eldorado

ENGINE TYPE:
V-twin

DISPLACEMENT:
844 cc (approx. 52 cubic inches)

VALVE TRAIN:
Overhead valves

CARBURETION:
Dell'Orto

TRANSMISSION:
Five-speed, foot shift

FRONT SUSPENSION:
Telescopic

FRONT BRAKE(S):
Drum

REAR SUSPENSION:
Swingarm with coil-over shocks

REAR BRAKE:
Drum

WEIGHT:
550 pounds

FINAL DRIVE:
Shaft

OWNER:
Joe Rybacek

Above: An 850 Eldorado is well-suited for use with a sidecar, its torquey V-twin able to put out plenty of low-end power. Note that the tires have a flat tread like those used on a car; since the sidecar didn't permit lean angles, the flat tread put more rubber on the road. *Far Left:* Dual horns trumpet a warning to fellow motorists.

1973
MOTO GUZZI V7 SPORT

Moto Guzzi began building motorcycles in 1920, and became known for its horizontal single-cylinder engines. Most displaced about 500 ccs, and though many Moto Guzzis had a sporting nature, none were really fast. Surprisingly, this design carried on for more than 45 years with only minor changes.

It wasn't until the mid-1960s that Moto Guzzi replaced the horizontal single with its now-famous V-twin. Mounted in a bike called the V7, this engine initially displaced 700 ccs, but was bumped to 750 ccs in 1969. The V7 used shaft drive in place of a chain, and when fitted with the proper accessories, made for an impressive touring mount.

In an effort to reach a more sporting audience, Moto Guzzi rolled out a trimmed-down version that was called—appropriately—the V7 Sport. A lower seat height and relatively flat handlebars resulted in a low riding position and low center of gravity, which, along with lighter bodywork, helped the V7 Sport hold true to its name.

YEAR:
1973

MANUFACTURER:
Moto Guzzi

MODEL:
V7 Sport

ENGINE TYPE:
V-twin

DISPLACEMENT:
748 cc (approx. 46 cubic inches)

VALVE TRAIN:
Overhead valves

CARBURETION:
Dell'Orto

TRANSMISSION:
Five-speed, foot shift

FRONT SUSPENSION:
Telescopic

FRONT BRAKE(S):
Drum

REAR SUSPENSION:
Swingarm with coil-over shocks

REAR BRAKE:
Drum

WEIGHT:
508 pounds

FINAL DRIVE:
Shaft

OWNER:
Joe Rybacek

To distinguish it from Moto Guzzi's similar touring-oriented models, the V7 Sport boasted thinner fenders, lower handlebars, smaller side covers that exposed more of the frame, and a sporting saddle with built-in backrest and rear fairing. Early models, such as the example shown, had a silver-painted frame; later models switched to basic black.

1974
MOTO GUZZI 850 L.A.P.D.

The Moto Guzzi had proven its abilities during the 1973 model year, and was chosen as the official Los Angeles Police Department mount in 1974. Mechanicals were unchanged for police use, but a mass of accessories were added.

The V-twin engine was a smooth, powerful choice for police duty, but the exposed cylinder heads were often hit by the patrolman's boot as he got on or off. As a result, heavy chrome guard rails were bolted to the valve covers to avoid damaging boots or cylinder heads.

Clustered around the certified speedometer were the usual indicator lights along with toggle switches for the siren and warning flashers. A pleated solo seat was used to provide additional comfort for those long days in the saddle, with floor boards and a heel/toe shift lever added to further alleviate discomfort for the mounted officers. The large, Harley-style windshield did an admirable job of deflecting insects and the occasional raindrop.

YEAR:
1974

MANUFACTURER:
Moto Guzzi

MODEL:
850 L.A.P.D.

ENGINE TYPE:
V-twin

DISPLACEMENT:
844 cc (approx. 52 cubic inches)

VALVE TRAIN:
Overhead valves

CARBURETION:
Dell'Orto

TRANSMISSION:
Five-speed, foot shift

FRONT SUSPENSION:
Telescopic

FRONT BRAKE(S):
Disc

REAR SUSPENSION:
Swingarm with coil-over shocks

REAR BRAKE:
Drum

WEIGHT:
550 pounds

FINAL DRIVE:
Shaft

OWNER:
Joe Rybacek

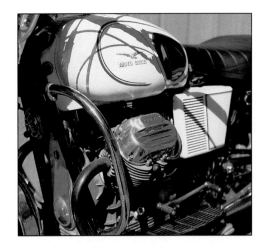

Left: Tall oblong cover that runs vertically in front of the engine hides the generator drive belt. Note that floorboards were used instead of foot pegs for all-day comfort. *Below:* L.A.P.D. bikes were equipped with solo seat, chromed fenders, and other special touches, such as valve-cover guards. Moto Guzzis were popular police bikes during the Seventies, but many were later replaced by more powerful, reliable Kawasaki 1000s.

1974
MZ TS250

As seldom as they are seen here in the states, MZs are popular overseas, as the company was the leading builder of motorcycles in Eastern Europe for many years. Not only were MZs popular with the masses, they were also accomplished in several arenas of racing, including trials and road circuits. Mike Hailwood rode a factory MZ race bike before his stint with Ducati.

First built in Zschopau, East Germany, the MZ TS250 is about what you would probably expect from the former Communist country. Looking at its street machine, one would never guess the company had any racing blood in its veins. Powered by a simple 250-cc, two-stroke engine, the TS250 is not about to set any speed records. And the cast fins on the cylinder head look a bit unfinished, but still do their job of dissipating heat.

Though silver paint substitutes for chrome plating on the fenders, the bulbous fuel tank is dressed to kill with its chrome side panels. Chrome plating was also applied to the large headlight nacelle, a component that is often painted body color.

Suspended with common underpinnings and slowed with nothing more than drum brakes, the MZ is a basic mount, but in the mid-Seventies, it dutifully filled its homeland's need for simple transportation.

YEAR:
1974

MANUFACTURER:
MZ

MODEL:
TS250

ENGINE TYPE:
Vertical single

DISPLACEMENT:
243 cc (approx. 15 cubic inches)

VALVE TRAIN:
Two-stroke

CARBURETION:
NA

TRANSMISSION:
Four-speed, foot shift

FRONT SUSPENSION:
Telescopic

FRONT BRAKE(S):
Drum

REAR SUSPENSION:
Swingarm with coil-over shocks

REAR BRAKE:
Drum

WEIGHT:
286 pounds

FINAL DRIVE:
Chain

OWNER:
Dick Cogswell

Left: Long forks, small front wheel, and boxy fuel tank give the TS250 an awkward stance. Note that the mirror is attached to the end of the handlebar. Oddly, the mirror and fenders are painted silver, while the tank side panel, air-cleaner cover, and headlight *(below)* are chromed. *Below left:* Single-cylinder two-stroke engine won't win any beauty awards, but sports huge cooling fins. *Bottom right:* Gas cap heralds the company's string of triumphs in the International Six Days trials event.

1974
RICKMAN/HONDA

Calling England its home, Rickman has been producing rolling motorcycle chassis since 1959, early efforts usually carrying engines from Triumph, AJS, or Matchless. Purchased by riders for both street and track applications, a Rickman chassis was designed to be a bolt-together affair, the package containing the frame, brakes, wheels, tires, and even the hand-laid fiberglass bodywork. A completed Rickman conversion would typically trim nearly 75 pounds from the stock motorcycle's curb weight.

In 1974, Rickman released its first frame kit for the Honda CB750. Combining a proven engine with a race-quality chassis made a Rickman/Honda a force to be reckoned with. The example shown here has been upgraded with Boranni wheels, Lockheed brakes, and a nickel-plated frame.

Modern advances in chassis design and construction have just about forced Rickman out of the market. However, examples of its early work can still be seen coupled to vintage classics around the world.

YEAR:
1974

MANUFACTURER:
Rickman/Honda

MODEL:
—

ENGINE TYPE:
Inline four

DISPLACEMENT:
750 cc (approx. 45 cubic inches)

VALVE TRAIN:
Overhead cam

CARBURETION:
NA

TRANSMISSION:
Five-speed, foot shift

FRONT SUSPENSION:
Telescopic

FRONT BRAKE(S):
Disc

REAR SUSPENSION:
Swingarm with coil-over shocks

REAR BRAKE:
Disc

WEIGHT:
NA

FINAL DRIVE:
Chain

OWNER:
Brad and Cindy Mobley

With a new frame and sleek fiberglass bodywork, it was often hard to tell what engine was powering a Rickman. This example carries a modified 750-cc Honda inline four, one of the more popular—and powerful—engines available at that time.

1975
HONDA GL1000

After showing the world what they could do with the CB750 in 1969, Honda was ready to do it again in 1975. When the GL1000 Gold Wing debuted that year, it was obvious Honda had become a leader in motorcycle technology.

Besides the unusual water-cooled "flat four" engine that displaced 999 ccs, the GL1000 came equipped with shaft drive. The "fuel tank" was nothing more than a cover for the electronics; the real tank was located between the two side covers for a lower center of gravity.

The price to be paid for all these features was weight. Without fairing, saddlebags, luggage, or rider, the GL1000 tipped the scales at a hefty 584 pounds.

In the first five years of production, Honda sold just under 100,000 copies of a motorcycle that would become a legend. The original Gold Wing has since grown into a six-cylinder, 1500-cc behemoth that comes complete with a reverse gear and more electronic amenities than the Space Shuttle.

YEAR:
1975

MANUFACTURER:
Honda

MODEL:
GL1000

ENGINE TYPE:
Horizontally opposed four

DISPLACEMENT:
999 cc (approx. 61 cubic inches)

VALVE TRAIN:
Overhead cam

CARBURETION:
NA

TRANSMISSION:
Five-speed, foot shift

FRONT SUSPENSION:
Telescopic

FRONT BRAKE(S):
Dual discs

REAR SUSPENSION:
Swingarm with coil-over shocks

REAR BRAKE:
Disc

WEIGHT:
584 pounds

FINAL DRIVE:
Shaft

OWNER:
Ray Landy

Honda's Gold Wing did to the touring market what the CB750 had done a few years before to the performance market. Rarely was a Gold Wing seen *au naturel* as shown here; they were usually loaded down with fairings, bags, and travel trunks. By that time, they typically tipped the scales at close to 700 pounds, so the torquey flat-four engine and triple disc brakes were much appreciated by riders.

1975
SUZUKI GT750

Long a producer of small- and medium-displacement two-stroke street bikes, Suzuki went out on a technological limb in 1971 and introduced the GT750. It became known as the "Water Buffalo" due to its large-displacement water-cooled two-stroke engine.

Being water cooled, the GT750 had a sizable radiator bolted to the front chassis downtubes. The engine's water jacket kept it cool and helped to reduce noise. The 738-cc three-cylinder engine dumped its spent exhaust into four separate pipes. Each of these had a full-length megaphone that was made up of two halves, with a distinct mechanical seam on both the top and bottom.

Despite all the technology, the GT750 was overshadowed by Kawasaki's two-stroke triples, which weren't water-cooled but were considerably quicker. Nevertheless, the Water Buffalo sold fairly well, and continued until 1977, when it was replaced by a "conventional" four-cylinder four-stroke.

YEAR:
1975

MANUFACTURER:
Suzuki

MODEL:
GT750

ENGINE TYPE:
Inline three

DISPLACEMENT:
738 cc (approx. 44 cubic inches)

VALVE TRAIN:
Two-stroke

CARBURETION:
NA

TRANSMISSION:
Five-speed, foot shift

FRONT SUSPENSION:
Telescopic

FRONT BRAKE(S):
Dual discs

REAR SUSPENSION:
Swingarm with coil-over shocks

REAR BRAKE:
Drum

WEIGHT:
524 pounds

FINAL DRIVE:
Chain

OWNER:
Pete Bollenbach

Suzuki's "Water Buffalo" wasn't your typical two-stroke motorcycle. At 738 ccs, the engine was about 50-percent larger than any production two-stroke before it, and water-cooled to boot—rare for any bike. Furthermore, most two-strokes were light; at 524 pounds, the GT750 was heavier than even Honda's 750 Four.

1975
TRIUMPH TRIDENT

In an attempt to fend off the attack of Japanese exports to the lucrative U.S. market, Triumph and BSA released a pair of three-cylinder models. The Triumph T150 Trident and BSA Rocket 3 were introduced in the states during the summer of 1968.

While both were considered decent motorcycles that challenged the best in terms of performance, their strengths paled with the introduction of Honda's 750 Four a few months later. Both British bikes received minor updates in subsequent years, but the Rocket 3 dropped out of the picture in 1973 (along with BSA itself), while the Trident got an overhaul.

Unfortunately for Triumph, the Superbike ante had been raised by the likes of Kawasaki's new Z-1, and though certainly improved, the Trident just didn't measure up. As a result, Triumph's triple faded from the scene after 1976, though the name was revived in 1990 for a more modern water-cooled three-cylinder machine that wasn't exported to the States.

YEAR:
1975

MANUFACTURER:
Triumph

MODEL:
Trident

ENGINE TYPE:
Inline three

DISPLACEMENT:
750 cc (approx. 45 cubic inches)

VALVE TRAIN:
Overhead valves

CARBURETION:
Amal

TRANSMISSION:
Four-speed, foot shift

FRONT SUSPENSION:
Telescopic

FRONT BRAKE(S):
Disc

REAR SUSPENSION:
Swingarm with coil-over shocks

REAR BRAKE:
Drum

WEIGHT:
503 pounds

FINAL DRIVE:
Chain

OWNER:
Matt Jonas

The second-generation Trident received some subtle changes, including an electric starter and cylinders that went from vertical to being slightly inclined. It also got a left-side shifter and front disc brake. But the Trident was overwhelmed by competitors, among them its own Bonneville twin-cylinder sibling that had grown to the same 750 ccs in 1973.

1976
HERCULES W2000

Looking back over the history of motorcycling, it's evident that a variety of power-plants have been used to propel the rolling chassis. From the very first steam-powered engines to the multi-valve electronic wonders of today, there was very little that wasn't attempted.

Hercules started building motorcycles with proprietary engines in 1903. A division of the giant Fichtel and Sachs Company, Hercules designed the chassis for the motorcycles bearing its name. After World War II, the company concentrated on building two-stroke machines that ranged from 48 to 248 ccs.

In an effort to combine efficiency and smooth power delivery, a Wankel engine was slipped into a Hercules frame. Powered by a Sachs 292-cc, single-rotor engine, the W2000 was the first commercially built Wankel-powered motorcycle.

The prototype W2000 had its engine mated to a BMW gearbox with shaft drive, but production versions got a different transmission and were chain-driven. While the Wankel was indeed a silky smooth powerplant, it generated excess heat and the W2000 was never sold in great numbers.

Another attempt at a Wankel-powered motorcycle was made by Suzuki. Featuring a water-cooled 500-cc single-rotor engine, the RE-5 proved to be unreliable and it too was quickly discontinued.

YEAR:
1976

MANUFACTURER:
Hercules

MODEL:
W2000

ENGINE TYPE:
Single-rotor Wankel

DISPLACEMENT:
292 cc (approx. 18 cubic inches)

VALVE TRAIN:
—

CARBURETION:
Bing

TRANSMISSION:
Six-speed, foot shift

FRONT SUSPENSION:
Telescopic

FRONT BRAKE(S):
Disc

REAR SUSPENSION:
Swingarm with coil-over shocks

REAR BRAKE:
Drum

WEIGHT:
NA

FINAL DRIVE:
Chain

OWNER:
Jim, Jeff, and Kevin Minnis

Far left: If the engine's appearance didn't give away the W2000's secret, the side-panel badge left no doubt. *Left:* Sachs rotary engine carried a large fan up front, but it wasn't enough to keep the wankel from overheating. Note the rather modest cooling fins, no doubt a contributing factor to the problem.

1976
HONDA CB400

After introducing the world to "popularly priced" four-cylinder motorcycles with the CB750 in 1969, Honda followed with a string of lighter fours with engines as small as 350 ccs. One of the most sporting of these was the CB400, introduced in 1975.

For the most part, the CB400 was simply an upgraded version of the 350 model from the previous year. The most striking change was the swoopy four-into-one exhaust system that snaked around the frame, converging into a single muffler on the right side of the bike. Also noticeable were the angular fuel tank, black side covers, and flat cafe-style handlebars, all of which gave the bike more of a racer-like look.

Although aimed at the sporting segment of the market, the CB400 came up a little short in the performance department compared to the competition, most notably the quick but noisy two-stroke triples from Kawasaki. But whatever the CB400's engine lacked in power it made up for in refinement, the small-displacement four-stroke being smooth and less audibly irritating than a two-stroke.

YEAR:
1976

MANUFACTURER:
Honda

MODEL:
CB400

ENGINE TYPE:
Inline four

DISPLACEMENT:
408 cc (approx. 25 cubic inches)

VALVE TRAIN:
Overhead cam

CARBURETION:
Keihin

TRANSMISSION:
Six-speed, foot shift

FRONT SUSPENSION:
Telescopic

FRONT BRAKE(S):
Disc

REAR SUSPENSION:
Swingarm with coil-over shocks

REAR BRAKE:
Drum

WEIGHT:
375 pounds

FINAL DRIVE:
Chain

OWNER:
Lee-Anne and Michael Shapiro

SUPER SPORT

The CB400 could out-handle most sporting machines of the era, though it couldn't keep up on the straights. The 408-cc inline four was backed by a six-speed transmission—something of a rarity at the time—which helped keep the high-winding engine in its powerband; redline *(left)* was a lofty 10,000 rpm.

1976
MOTO GUZZI V1000 CONVERT

After boosting its V-twin from 700 ccs to 750 ccs and then 850 ccs, Moto Guzzi made the jump to a full liter. One of the first recipients of the bigger engine was a new model called the V1000 Convert.

"Convert" stood for converter—as in torque converter. Power was fed from the engine through a torque converter to a conventional clutch. Though the big Guzzi still used a transmission, it had only two speeds. The clutch had to be disengaged to manually shift between low and high gear, but thanks to the torque converter, the rider could come to a complete stop in either gear, and then accelerate away without touching the clutch or the gearshift lever.

By this time, many of the company's products were focused on the sport-touring market, but the V1000 Convert was never considered as such. It was a touring machine, pure and simple, and in that capacity had much to offer.

YEAR:
1976

MANUFACTURER:
Moto Guzzi

MODEL:
V1000 Convert

ENGINE TYPE:
V-twin

DISPLACEMENT:
1000 cc (approx. 61 cubic inches)

VALVE TRAIN:
Overhead valves

CARBURETION:
Dell'Orto

TRANSMISSION:
Two-speed with torque converter

FRONT SUSPENSION:
Telescopic

FRONT BRAKE(S):
Dual discs

REAR SUSPENSION:
Swingarm with coil-over shocks

REAR BRAKE:
Disc

WEIGHT:
572 pounds

FINAL DRIVE:
Shaft

OWNER:
Jim, Jeff, and Kevin Minnis

Tipping the scales at nearly 600 pounds, the V1000 Convert was not well-suited to fast cornering. Furthermore, the two-speed transmission and torque converter resulted in leisurely acceleration, so the V1000 Convert was more at home on long tours than on twisty road courses. *Below:* Dashboard held all kinds of warning lights, but no tachometer. *Bottom:* Gear selection was made through a "heel-and-toe" lever.

1976
NORTON COMMANDO

Norton's Commando series bowed in 1968 to great fanfare, but by the mid-Seventies had grown long in the tooth. Originally offered with a 750-cc engine, it was decided that a power boost was in order to help stem the tide of the Japanese onslaught.

The engine itself was going on 30 years old, but it was a solid design, and Norton increased its displacement to 829 ccs in what would turn out to be its final incarnation. Along with the larger engine came a front disc brake, joined later by a rear disc.

Despite these efforts, Norton found itself deeper and deeper in financial muck. Merged with AJS and Matchless back in the Sixties, Norton was folded in with BSA and Triumph in the Seventies. BSA dropped out after 1973, leaving Triumph and Norton to soldier on alone. They didn't march very far.

Though Triumph struggled for a few years afterward, Norton ceased production in 1977. However, both marques made cameo appearances during the Eighties, Norton fielding a rotary-engined model that was produced in small numbers.

YEAR:
1976

MANUFACTURER:
Norton

MODEL:
Commando

ENGINE TYPE:
Vertical twin

DISPLACEMENT:
829 cc (approx. 50 cubic inches)

VALVE TRAIN:
Overhead valves

CARBURETION:
NA

TRANSMISSION:
Four-speed, foot shift

FRONT SUSPENSION:
Telescopic

FRONT BRAKE(S):
Disc

REAR SUSPENSION:
Swingarm with coil-over shocks

REAR BRAKE:
Disc

WEIGHT:
NA

FINAL DRIVE:
Chain

OWNER:
Rick Weber

By 1976, the Commando sported front and rear disc brakes, U.S.-spec left-side shift, and electric starting—features earlier bikes lacked that made them less attractive to American riders. Furthermore, the seat was now hinged for convenience, and the speedometer and tach were joined by a warning-light console *(above)*.

1976
TRIUMPH BONNEVILLE

Almost the entire history of Triumph has been tainted by financial strife. The influx of high-performance, low-cost Japanese rivals in the Seventies only intensified the problems.

Due to the cash-strapped position of the company, changes to the T140V Bonneville for 1976 were few. The drum brake on the rear wheel was finally replaced with a modern disc, and in a desperate attempt to conform to the tastes of the all-important U.S. market, the gear-shift lever was moved to the left side of the engine where Americans were used to finding it. The rubber fork gaitors were not usually seen on European-spec Bonnevilles, but were standard equipment on T140s bound for the U.S. Color choices were restricted to blue or red with white accent panels.

As a historical landmark, the 1976 Bonnevilles were the first to be built under the new Meriden financial cooperative. The cooperative folded in 1983, but the Bonneville stumbled on into 1988, the final years of production being handled by Les Harris under license from Triumph.

YEAR:
1976

MANUFACTURER:
Triumph

MODEL:
Bonneville

ENGINE TYPE:
Vertical twin

DISPLACEMENT:
750 cc (approx. 45 cubic inches)

VALVE TRAIN:
Overhead valves

CARBURETION:
Amal

TRANSMISSION:
Five-speed, foot shift

FRONT SUSPENSION:
Telescopic

FRONT BRAKE(S):
Disc

REAR SUSPENSION:
Swingarm with coil-over shocks

REAR BRAKE:
Disc

WEIGHT:
NA

FINAL DRIVE:
Chain

OWNER:
Joe Rybacek

Japanese motorcycles typically mounted the shift lever on the left side of the bike, and Harley-Davidson moved it there in the early Seventies. Triumph didn't make the switch until 1976, so riders of earlier models who were not accustomed to English ways often downshifted the transmission when they were trying to go for the brake pedal—sometimes with disastrous results. Along with the left-side shifter, the '76 Bonneville had front and rear disc brakes, but otherwise had changed little in appearance since the late Sixties.

1976
TRITON

Although not a factory effort, the Triton was a common sight in the 1960s. By combining a Triumph powerplant with a Norton chassis, one could build a machine that was ready for use either on track or off.

This particular Triton features a Triumph 750-cc engine with a five-speed gearbox. However, the engine most often chosen was a 650-cc powerplant from a Bonneville.

The stock Norton featherbed chassis is of 1966 vintage. Up front, a set of Ceriani forks provide contemporary suspension travel and compliance. Both the fuel and oil tanks are fabricated from highly polished aluminum and help to keep the weight of the Triton below 400 pounds.

In the past, Tritons such as this one were a common sight circulating the great tracks in Europe. Often the entry of a privateer, the Triton did an admirable job of keeping pace with the factory racers.

YEAR:
1976

MANUFACTURER:
Triton

MODEL:
—

ENGINE TYPE:
Vertical twin

DISPLACEMENT:
750 cc (approx. 45 cubic inches)

VALVE TRAIN:
Overhead valves

CARBURETION:
NA

TRANSMISSION:
Five-speed, foot shift

FRONT SUSPENSION:
Telescopic

FRONT BRAKE(S):
Drum

REAR SUSPENSION:
Swingarm with coil-over shocks

REAR BRAKE:
Drum

WEIGHT:
NA

FINAL DRIVE:
Chain

OWNER:
Thom Search

Left: Triumph engines came stock with Amal carburetors, but these were often replaced with high-performance Mikuni smoothbores, as found on this example. *Below:* Decal on the polished aluminum fuel tank is a clever combination of the scripts used in Triumph and Norton logos. The seat is from a Norton Manx racer, adding to the competition flavor of the bike.

1977
DUCATI 900SS

Ducati's domination on the racetracks across Europe has led to the development of some exceptional road-going machines. With the debut of the 750S with its desmodromic valvetrain, Ducati reached a new plateau of performance. Able to reach 120 miles per hour in a single bound, the 750S reintroduced the world to Italian Superbikes.

In November of 1973, Ducati rolled out its next weapon. The 860GT boasted a larger engine that pushed the performance envelope even further, and it was this platform that launched the 900SS in 1976.

With a top speed of over 140 miles per hour, the 900SS was as fast as anything the Japanese had to offer. The carefully sculpted steel fuel tank was surrounded by a bullet-shaped half fairing, and the solo saddle was backed by an aerodynamic tailpiece. Together, these elements created a true racing image for the 900SS, which was only strengthened when Mike Hailwood rode a race-prepped version to victory at the Isle of Man TT.

YEAR:
1977

MANUFACTURER:
Ducati

MODEL:
900SS

ENGINE TYPE:
V-twin

DISPLACEMENT:
860 cc (approx. 53 cubic inches)

VALVE TRAIN:
Overhead cam with desmodromic valve actuation

CARBURETION:
NA

TRANSMISSION:
Five-speed, foot shift

FRONT SUSPENSION:
Telescopic

FRONT BRAKE(S):
Dual discs

REAR SUSPENSION:
Swingarm with coil-over shocks

REAR BRAKE:
Disc

WEIGHT
425 pounds

FINAL DRIVE:
Chain

OWNER:
Barbara Liles and Warren Dorn

Left: Ducati's V-twin engine, introduced in 1971, carried the company's famed desmodromic valve actuation, which closes the valves mechanically rather than with springs; this virtually eliminates high-rpm valve float. Note that the cooling fins on the forward cylinder run in a different direction than those on the rear cylinder due to the direction of air flow. *Above:* Issued in Thailand, wording across the top of the license plate reads "Bangkok, Great City."

1977
HARLEY-DAVIDSON MX250

In the late 1960s, motocross racing started to catch on in the U.S. Although largely ignored at first, interest steadily grew and the AMA eventually recognized it as a sanctioned event.

Once the AMA had given its blessing, Harley-Davidson decided to try its hand at building a motocross machine. About 100 MX250s were built in 1976 for the purpose of on-track development. They were brought to the showroom the following year.

Built by Harley's Italian partner, Aermacchi, the MX250 was powered by a single-cylinder two-stroke engine of 249-cc displacement. A strong, light, chrome-moly frame was used, along with remote-reservoir rear shocks.

Unfortunately, Harley's timing could not have been much worse. As good as the MX250 was, Japanese manufacturers began flooding the market with more capable machinery that sold for less, and the MX250 was discontinued after 1978.

YEAR:
1977

MANUFACTURER:
Harley-Davidson

MODEL:
MX250

ENGINE TYPE:
Vertical single

DISPLACEMENT:
249 cc (approx. 15 cubic inches)

VALVE TRAIN:
Two-stroke

CARBURETION:
Dell'Orto

TRANSMISSION:
Five-speed, foot shift

FRONT SUSPENSION:
Telescopic

FRONT BRAKE(S):
Drum

REAR SUSPENSION:
Swingarm with coil-over shocks

REAR BRAKE:
Drum

WEIGHT:
233 pounds

FINAL DRIVE:
Chain

OWNER:
Illinois Harley-Davidson

Above: Sold by Harley-Davidson dealers but built by Harley's Italian partner Aermacchi using Kayaba forks and wheels made by Yamaha of Japan, the MX250 was truly an international exercise. *Left:* Plastic front fender was embossed with the H-D logo. *Far left:* All-important kill switch was mounted by the left hand grip.

1977
MV AGUSTA 750S AMERICA

MV Agusta is one of the oldest and most respected names in motorcycling history. During its heyday, MV claimed 37 Manufacturer's World Championships and stood on the top step of the winner's circle at the end of 270 Gran Prix races.

The 790-cc engine in the 750S America has its roots in the 500-cc GP powerplant, but then most of MV's machines have racing blood in their veins. Arturo Magni was the man responsible for nearly all of MV's racing success, and when his designs were put into the hands of riders like Mike Hailwood, the competition had little hope of winning.

The sleek half-fairing is a popular Magni accessory and was also available in a full GP configuration. Weighing 507 pounds without fluids, the 750S is no lightweight, but its handling at speed belies the mass. The suede-covered racing saddle does its best to keep the pilot in place during the kind of spirited cornering maneuvers the 750S is so adept at performing.

YEAR:
1977

MANUFACTURER:
MV Agusta

MODEL:
750S America

ENGINE TYPE:
Inline four

DISPLACEMENT:
790 cc (approx. 48 cubic inches)

VALVE TRAIN:
Double overhead cams

CARBURETION:
Dell'Orto

TRANSMISSION:
Five-speed, foot shift

FRONT SUSPENSION:
Telescopic

FRONT BRAKE(S):
Dual discs

REAR SUSPENSION:
Swingarm with coil-over shocks

REAR BRAKE:
Drum

WEIGHT
507 pounds

FINAL DRIVE:
Shaft

OWNER:
Jim Rau

When shipped from the factory, the 750S America came equipped with an exhaust system that consisted of chrome downtubes flowing into megaphone mufflers finished with black crinkle paint. This bike wears headers designed by Arturo Magni, MV's racing guru. *Left:* Due to their limited production, MVs sport many parts machined from lightweight metals that on other bikes are made from cast metal or molded plastic.

1978
HARLEY-DAVIDSON FXS

Harley-Davidson's first "factory custom" was released in 1971, setting the stage for many more to follow. Called the FX Super Glide, it combined the frame and engine from the big FL-series twins with the front forks and other trim pieces from the XL Sportster—hence the FX designation.

In the middle of 1977, Harley rolled out the FXS Low Rider. Like the Super Glide, it was based on the big FL series frame with a 74-cubic-inch V-twin engine. It contrasted sharply with Harley's other new entry for 1977, the XLCR. While the Sportster-based XLCR was square and sporty, the FXS had a low, muscular flow to its sheetmetal.

In 1978, the Super Glide's first full year of production, it outsold all other models in Harley's catalog, accounting for nearly 20 percent of total sales. The FXS was initially sold only in metallic gray with orange script, but black and white were offered late in the model year.

On the FXS, fuel is stored in the split "Fat Bob" tanks, which give the bike a substantial look. The 1978 version still carried both kick and electric starters, and the final drive was handled with a multi-row chain.

Though it was the first year for the Low Rider, 1978 turned out to be the last year for the venerable 74-cubic-inch V-twin. Harley increased the displacement to 80 cubic inches for 1979, where it remains to this day.

YEAR:
1978

MANUFACTURER:
Harley-Davidson

MODEL:
FXS

ENGINE TYPE:
V-twin

DISPLACEMENT:
74 cubic inches

VALVE TRAIN:
Overhead valves

CARBURETION:
Keihin

TRANSMISSION:
Four-speed, foot shift

FRONT SUSPENSION:
Telescopic

FRONT BRAKE(S):
Dual discs

REAR SUSPENSION:
Swingarm with coil-over shocks

REAR BRAKE:
Disc

WEIGHT:
NA

FINAL DRIVE:
Chain

OWNER:
Ted Moran

Continuing the formula used for the original Super Glide of 1971, the first Low Rider featured the frame and engine from the FL-series "Big Twins" supported by the front end of the smaller XL series. *Left:* Note the huge battery used to turn over the 74-cubic-inch V-twin. A matte-black finish was used on the instrument panel and upper tank trim *(lower left)* while braking was handled by dual discs in front and a single disc at the rear *(lower right).*

1978
KAWASAKI Z1-R

Kawasaki's 900-cc four-cylinder Z-1 of 1973 set new standards for motorcycle performance, yet company officials were soon discussing the idea of building a "special" version of the successful model. Since the cafe-racer look was in vogue at the time, the decision was made to create their own variation.

Using existing blueprints for the soon-to-be-released KZ1000, the Z1-R was intended to be little more than a styling exercise. The fuel tank was drawn up using flat, angular lines that were mimicked by the triangular side panels and sharply creased front fender. The fiberglass fairing followed suit, and all the bodywork was sprayed with specially blended Ice Blue metallic paint that was used only on the Z1-R.

The frame was the same as the original Z-1 of 1973, but several improvements were made to compliment the exclusive nature of the R model. Its 1015-cc engine exhausted through the industry's first factory-installed four-into-one header system, while triple disc brakes with drilled rotors redefined stopping power.

Extensive use of fiberglass for the body components helped reduce weight, and combined with the free-breathing nature of the engine, allowed the Z1-R to become the first stock street bike to record sub-12-second runs in the standing-start quarter-mile. Styling exercise indeed.

YEAR:
1978

MANUFACTURER:
Kawasaki

MODEL:
Z1-R

ENGINE TYPE:
Inline four

DISPLACEMENT:
1015 cc (approx. 62 cubic inches)

VALVE TRAIN:
Double overhead cams

CARBURETION:
Mikuni

TRANSMISSION:
Five-speed, foot shift

FRONT SUSPENSION:
Telescopic

FRONT BRAKE(S):
Dual discs

REAR SUSPENSION:
Swingarm with coil-over shocks

REAR BRAKE:
Disc

WEIGHT:
570 pounds

FINAL DRIVE:
Chain

OWNER:
Jim Goebel

With its chiseled lines, bikini fairing, and special Ice Blue paint, the Z1-R stood out in a crowd. And on the road, the R's 1015-cc twin-cam four exhausting through four-into-one headers allowed it to leave other Superbikes of the era in its wake. With that kind of speed potential, the triple disc brakes with drilled rotors were a welcome addition.

1978
MOTO GUZZI LEMANS

When Moto Guzzi introduced its V-twin engine in the mid-1960s, it displaced 700 ccs and was mounted in a shaft-drive model called the V7. This engine soon grew to 750 ccs, and a performance-oriented V7 Sport version followed.

Nineteen seventy-two brought a new frame and a front-mounted alternator to replace the top-mounted generator. A couple of years later the V-twin was boosted to 850 ccs, then to 1000.

By this time, the V7 Sport had fallen by the wayside, and Moto Guzzi wanted to bring out a new sport model to capture the attention of the enthusiast market. Armed with an 850-cc version of the venerable V-twin, the LeMans Mk I was introduced in 1976.

Unique to the LeMans were clip-on handle bars, bikini fairing, and distinct badging and trim. Though not in the same performance league as Japanese Superbikes, the LeMans offered a unique blend of V-twin torque and Italian style, and would remain in production for some time to come.

YEAR:
1978

MANUFACTURER:
Moto Guzzi

MODEL:
LeMans

ENGINE TYPE:
V-twin

DISPLACEMENT:
844 cc (approx. 52 cubic inches)

VALVE TRAIN:
Overhead valves

CARBURETION:
Dell'Orto

TRANSMISSION:
Five-speed, foot shift

FRONT SUSPENSION:
Telescopic

FRONT BRAKE(S):
Dual discs

REAR SUSPENSION:
Swingarm with coil-over shocks

REAR BRAKE:
Disc

WEIGHT
436 pounds

FINAL DRIVE:
Shaft

OWNER:
Barbara Liles and Warren Dorn

Like other Moto Guzzis of the period, the LeMans was built on a tubular frame, a section of which could be unbolted to allow for easy removal of the engine. It also had a linked braking system where the foot pedal controlled not only the rear disc, but also one of the twin front discs; the other was activated by the conventional hand-brake lever. *Opposite page:* LeMans exhaust system featured a balance pipe that snaked beneath the alternator at the front of the engine.

1981
BMW R65

Buyers admiring BMW's long-standing reputation for building dependable machines found that it came at a price—a rather high price. So in 1979, BMW built the R65 as an entry-level model for those otherwise unable to afford the cost of admission.

Powered by a 650-cc version of BMW's traditional horizontally opposed twin, the R65 was really just a scaled-down version of the company's larger 1000-cc model. As a result, what was lost in sheer power was replaced with manageability; weighing in at only 452 pounds with a full tank of fuel, the R65 was more nimble at low speeds.

Although identical to the original R65 in appearance, the 1981 version boasted several improvements. All BMWs that year gained transistorized ignitions to replace the old points-and-condenser systems. Cast sleeves were discarded in favor of Nikasil coating for the cylinders, and the intake and exhaust valves were enlarged to improve breathing. Oil pan capacity was also increased.

Despite all the improvements, the 1981 models carried a list price that was $235 less than the year before, allowing more hopeful BMW enthusiasts to walk into their local dealer and ride home on a new R65.

YEAR:
1981

MANUFACTURER:
BMW

MODEL:
R65

ENGINE TYPE:
Horizontally opposed twin

DISPLACEMENT:
650 cc (approx. 40 cubic inches)

VALVE TRAIN:
Overhead valves

CARBURETION:
Bing

TRANSMISSION:
Five-speed, foot shift

FRONT SUSPENSION:
Telescopic

FRONT BRAKE(S):
Dual discs

REAR SUSPENSION:
Swingarm with coil-over shocks

REAR BRAKE:
Drum

WEIGHT:
452 pounds

FINAL DRIVE:
Shaft

OWNER:
Michael Aldrich

Despite its mission as a low-cost, entry-level model, the R65 carried traditional BMW virtues. Twin disc brakes slowed the front wheel, while the rear drum was beautifully integrated into the cast rear wheel *(above right)*. Like most BMWs of the era, the R65's flat-twin engine was fed by a pair of Bing carburetors *(left)*.

1981
DUCATI HAILWOOD REPLICA

Mike Hailwood began his racing career at the tender age of 18. Initially riding for the MZ Gran Prix team, "Mike the Bike" would later switch to riding for Ducati. During his career, he would chalk up nine world championships and claim victory in over 70 Gran Prix events. It seems only fitting that the replica built to commemorate his success would turn out to be Ducati's best-selling model in the early Eighties.

Cloaked in the familiar red, white, and green of the Italian flag, the replica looks every inch a race bike. The GP-style front fairing is a one-piece ordeal that was later divided into two sections to allow for simpler access to the hardware that lurked within.

The race-proven 860-cc V-twin engine, complete with desmodromic valve train, seems right at home in the traditional Ducati birdcage chassis. The flowing two-into-one exhaust exits on the left side of the bike, and does little to mask the raucous note put out by the engine.

The extremely short clip-on handlebars help to fulfill the illusion of riding a true GP machine, but make parking a nightmare. Hidden beneath the fiberglass tail section is a spot reserved for a brave and durable riding partner since comfort is not a consideration on a race machine—or a replica.

YEAR:
1981

MANUFACTURER:
Ducati

MODEL:
Hailwood Replica

ENGINE TYPE:
V-twin

DISPLACEMENT:
860 cc (approx. 53 cubic inches)

VALVE TRAIN:
Overhead cam with desmodromic valve actuation

CARBURETION:
Dell'Orto

TRANSMISSION:
Five-speed, foot shift

FRONT SUSPENSION:
Telescopic

FRONT BRAKE(S):
Dual discs

REAR SUSPENSION:
Swingarm with coil-over shocks

REAR BRAKE:
Disc

WEIGHT:
NA

FINAL DRIVE:
Chain

OWNER:
Pete Bollenbach

Top left: Ducati's unique desmodromic valve actuation system is driven by a single over-head camshaft. Unlike most other OHC engines, which use a chain to spin the cam, Ducati used a shaft and bevel gears; this example carries a window through which the motion can be viewed. *Bottom left:* Fuel tank is fitted with a racing-inspired gas cap and vent/overflow tube. Tachometer indicates a redline of 8000 rpm—quite high for a large-displacement twin.

1981
HONDA CBX

Honda's mighty CBX was introduced in 1978 amidst a chorus of technical fanfare. While it was not the first motorcycle to be powered by a six-cylinder engine, it was the latest and arguably the most advanced entry into the hotly contested Superbike battle being fought by the Japanese manufacturers.

Even with its impressive brawn and intimidating six-pipe exhaust system, the CBX never really caught on with the street-racing crowd. Some competitors were cheaper, lighter, and (most importantly) quicker, so the big Honda was often dismissed as being more show than go.

Failing to capture its intended audience, Honda switched gears and headed the CBX into the Sport Touring category. Adding a sleek faring and custom-fitted saddle bags transformed the six-cylinder machine into an impressive road bike, its buttery-smooth engine affording effortless cruising at better than 100 mph. Yet despite its touring credentials, the CBX "dresser" didn't fare much better than its stripped-down predecessor, and production of Honda's six-cylinder wonder ceased at the end of the 1982 model year.

YEAR:
1981

MANUFACTURER:
Honda

MODEL:
CBX

ENGINE TYPE:
Inline six

DISPLACEMENT:
1047 cc (approx. 64 cubic inches)

VALVE TRAIN:
Double overhead cams

CARBURETION:
Keihin

TRANSMISSION:
Five-speed, foot shift

FRONT SUSPENSION:
Air-adjustable hydraulic

FRONT BRAKE(S):
Dual discs

REAR SUSPENSION:
Swingarm with air-adjustable coil-over shock

REAR BRAKE:
Disc

WEIGHT:
680 pounds

FINAL DRIVE:
Chain

OWNER:
Matt Jonas

Top left: CBX's signature was its waterfall of gleaming exhaust pipes. Rear saddlebags could be detached and carried like a briefcase. *Left:* Small "ducktail" spoiler on the front fender between the fork tubes directed air over the oil cooler and 24-valve heads. *Top right:* Due to government regulations in force at the time, the speedometer only registered to 85 mph—which the CBX could easily exceed in third gear.

1982
HARLEY-DAVIDSON FXB

For over half a century, the annual trek to the Black Hills of South Dakota has been a ritual for many motorcycle enthusiasts. One week each summer, the town of Sturgis teems with motorcyclists from around the country, and in 1982, Harley-Davidson decided to commemorate the event with the release of the FXB Sturgis.

As denoted by the nomenclature, the FXB is based on the Low Rider chassis and engine. The big difference is the "B" suffix, which in this instance stands for belts; both the primary and final drives are fitted with toothed belts in lieu of the typical chains. Although more difficult to repair, the dual belt system provides clean, quiet, and mostly trouble-free operation. Starting of the FXB can be accomplished by either pushing a button or kicking a lever. An electronic ignition alleviated some earlier problems, making the big twin easier to fire up.

The Sturgis is clothed in black with just enough chrome and color to make things interesting. A two-inch extension of the front forks gives it a "chopper" look. The dual fuel tanks are topped with a speedometer, tachometer, and matching filler caps. Like virtually all of Harley's early customs, the Sturgis is now a collector's piece. Unlike some of the others, however, it was a hit right from the start.

YEAR:
1982

MANUFACTURER:
Harley-Davidson

MODEL:
FXB

ENGINE TYPE:
V-twin

DISPLACEMENT:
80 cubic inches

VALVE TRAIN:
Overhead valves

CARBURETION:
Keihin

TRANSMISSION:
Four-speed, foot shift

FRONT SUSPENSION:
Telescopic

FRONT BRAKE(S):
Dual discs

REAR SUSPENSION:
Swingarm with coil-over shocks

REAR BRAKE:
Disc

WEIGHT:
590 pounds

FINAL DRIVE:
Belt

OWNER:
Rick Bernard

Opposite page: Sturgis models came equipped from the factory with a small leather pouch mounted behind the backrest. The pouch was often removed by owners. *Left:* Dual fuel tanks are made to look like one through the use of a black trim plate that runs up between them and surrounds the gauge panel.

1982
KAWASAKI KZ1000R

During the Seventies, Japanese manufacturers were turning out some impressive machines for the consumer. At about the same time, a man named Eddie Lawson was turning out some impressive lap times on his 250-cc race bike. When the Superbike class was created, Mr. Lawson found himself mounted on a bright green Kawasaki that often took him to the winner's podium.

Taking advantage of its racing success, Kawasaki created the KZ1000R, otherwise known as the Eddie Lawson Replica. Based on a standard KZ1000, it carried both cosmetic and mechanical alterations that set it apart from the Superbike crowd.

While the bikini fairing did little to protect the rider from the elements, it looked just right when viewed along with the black-painted engine and gold-accented cast wheels. In the performance department, Kerker four-into-one headers let the engine breathe freely, while an oil cooler was added to keep things from getting too hot.

For more serious racers, Kawasaki also offered a KZ1000S1. Intended for track use only, it was successfully campaigned by many private racers.

YEAR:
1982

MANUFACTURER:
Kawasaki

MODEL:
KZ1000R

ENGINE TYPE:
Inline four

DISPLACEMENT:
1015 cc (approx. 62 cubic inches)

VALVE TRAIN:
Double overhead cams

CARBURETION:
Keihin

TRANSMISSION:
Five-speed, foot shift

FRONT SUSPENSION:
Telescopic

FRONT BRAKE(S):
Dual discs

REAR SUSPENSION:
Swingarm with coil-over shocks

REAR BRAKE:
Disc

WEIGHT:
NA

FINAL DRIVE:
Chain

OWNER:
Al Pinkus

Above: Header manufacturer Kerker got equal billing on the KZ1000R's fuel tank. The company name was also emblazoned on the muffler that was fed by a four-into-one header. *Left:* Gold-colored "piggyback" reservoir shocks helped keep the rear tire on the road. *Far left:* Gauges were set in an automotive-style instrument panel; tachometer indicates a 9000-rpm redline.

1983
HONDA CX650T

Introduced to the raging Sportbike battle that was taking place in the early Eighties was a new and innovative competitor: the Honda CX500 Turbo. It was the world's first turbocharged production bike, featuring fuel injection and a radical fairing. The Turbo's powerplant was based on the water-cooled V-twin used in the shaft-drive CX500 introduced a few years earlier.

In 1983, both versions of the V-twin were bumped to 650 ccs. For the new CX650 Turbo, that meant a boost from 77 to 97 horsepower, making it one of the more powerful motorcycles available that year.

With their complex fuel injection systems and related sensors and actuators, the CX Turbos carried high prices and were a nightmare for shade-tree mechanics. Furthermore, many insurers assessed them with exorbitant premiums. So although the whistle of the turbo and resulting kick of acceleration boiled the adrenaline of those who rode one, the CX650 Turbo—along with the imitators that soon followed—sadly suffered a premature extinction.

YEAR:
1983

MANUFACTURER:
Honda

MODEL:
CX650T

ENGINE TYPE:
V-twin

DISPLACEMENT:
647 cc (approx. 40 cubic inches)

VALVE TRAIN:
Overhead valves

CARBURETION:
Fuel injection

TRANSMISSION:
Five speed, foot shift

FRONT SUSPENSION:
Telescopic

FRONT BRAKE(S):
Dual discs

REAR SUSPENSION:
Swingarm with coil-over shock

REAR BRAKE:
Disc

WEIGHT:
518 pounds

FINAL DRIVE:
Shaft

OWNER:
Matt Jonas

The original Honda CX500, introduced in the mid-Seventies, was a rather pedestrian ride, but featured a unique water-cooled V-twin with four pushrod-actuated valves per cylinder that was mounted across the frame (*á la* Moto Guzzi). It also had shaft drive and was one of the first bikes to use mag-style wheels. The Turbo version that followed in 1982 was the first turbocharged production bike and also featured fuel injection—another innovation. For 1983, the engine grew to 650 ccs, and the color scheme was changed from pearlescent eggshell with red and black accents to pearlescent white with red and blue trim as shown on our featured bike. *Left:* High-pressured pushrod twin redlined at an impressive 9000 rpm.

1984
BMW R65 LS

Once sales of the R65 began to accelerate, BMW did the next sensible thing: The price of the entry-level Beemer was lowered two years in a row, bringing the cost even closer to the Japanese 650s. Since the need for a motorcycle of this type was now proven, BMW drew up plans for a limited-edition version of the R65.

The resulting R65 LS was identical to its sibling in many ways, both carrying the same twin-cylinder boxer engine. The most outward change on the LS was the fork-mounted nacelle fairing. BMW claimed that front-end lift was reduced by 30 percent at high speeds with the fairing in place, and it also provided the rider a modicum of protection from the wind.

At the other end of the LS was a new molded tail section with integrated passenger grab rails. Lifting the dual saddle revealed a small storage compartment. Wider alloy wheels completed the cosmetic changes on the LS.

Along with the revisions came the usual BMW qualities. The low center of gravity offered by the boxer engine helped to provide nimble yet stable handling at all speeds, along with the crisp, light steering for which BMWs were well-known.

YEAR:
1984

MANUFACTURER:
BMW

MODEL:
R65 LS

ENGINE TYPE:
Horizontally opposed twin

DISPLACEMENT:
650 cc (approx. 40 cubic inches)

VALVE TRAIN:
Overhead valves

CARBURETION:
Bing

TRANSMISSION:
Five-speed, foot shift

FRONT SUSPENSION:
Telescopic

FRONT BRAKE(S):
Dual discs

REAR SUSPENSION:
Swingarm with coil-over shocks

REAR BRAKE:
Disc

WEIGHT:
425 pounds

FINAL DRIVE:
Shaft

OWNER:
Barbara Liles and Warren Dorn

Unusual handlebar fairing mounted the instruments in tall pods that blocked some of the wind hitting the rider's chest. Though the R65 was not as quick as most Japanese 650s, its triple disc brakes provided plenty of stopping power.

1984
LAVERDA RGS 1000

Since motorcycles represent only a small fraction of the output of the Laverda firm, those that do roll off the production line tend to be niche vehicles. As such, they don't have to appeal to a large audience—and don't try to. However, in an effort to sell more of their machines in the United States, the RGS 1000 was drawn with American tastes in mind while maintaining a distinct European flavor.

RG Studio (RGS) was responsible for the sleek bodywork. The rear cowling provides a method of limiting the rider's movement under hard acceleration. It can be removed to reveal the passenger's portion of the seat for two-up riding.

As often happens to offerings from Italy, models sold by the competition were more widely accepted by the market. As a result, the RGS 1000 didn't sell in great quantities—but then, niche vehicles rarely do.

YEAR:
1984

MANUFACTURER:
Laverda

MODEL:
RGS 1000

ENGINE TYPE:
Inline three

DISPLACEMENT:
981 cc (approx. 60 cubic inches)

VALVE TRAIN:
Double overhead cams

CARBURETION:
Dell'Orto

TRANSMISSION:
Five-speed, foot shift

FRONT SUSPENSION:
Telescopic

FRONT BRAKE(S):
Dual discs

REAR SUSPENSION:
Swingarm with coil-over shocks

REAR BRAKE:
Disc

WEIGHT:
556 pounds

FINAL DRIVE:
Chain

OWNER:
Michael H. Short

By 1984, Laverda's time-tested vertical triple boasted a new 120-degree crankshaft that smoothed out the power flow, but it still turned within sand-cast cases. Otherwise, the RGS 1000 was nicely finished, boasting a fairing that was integrated with the fuel tank, and a one-piece side cover that flowed into a removeable tailpiece. A back-bone frame configuration allowed for easier access to the top end of the engine, while the square-section swingarm provided additional rigidity for the rear suspension.

1985
YAMAHA RZ 500

In the early 1980s, the marketing department at Yamaha sensed the need for an all-out performance machine. It had to be light in weight, look and behave like a Gran Prix bike, and be within budgetary guidelines. After several years of development, the RZ 500 shot out of the Yamaha factory doors.

In a brash deviation from the norm, the RZ was powered by a 499-cc V-four two-stroke engine with twin cranks and liquid cooling. Somewhat more conventional was a chassis formed from square-section aluminum-alloy tubing. This choice of material allowed for superb stiffness matched with light weight.

The RZ's extraordinary performance and handling were actually seen as detriments to the average rider, and sales of Yamaha's little pocket rocket were poor. Placed in the proper hands, it was a potent weapon on the track, but unfortunately a handful around town. Furthermore, the two-stroke powerplant excluded the RZ 500 from the list of machines available for sale in the U.S., though several examples managed to find their way in anyhow.

YEAR:
1985

MANUFACTURER:
Yamaha

MODEL:
RZ 500

ENGINE TYPE:
V-four with dual crankshafts

DISPLACEMENT:
499 cc (approx. 30 cubic inches)

VALVE TRAIN:
Two-stroke

CARBURETION:
Mikuni

TRANSMISSION:
Six-speed, foot shift

FRONT SUSPENSION:
Telescopic

FRONT BRAKE(S):
Dual discs

REAR SUSPENSION:
Swingarm with coil-over shock

REAR BRAKE:
Disc

WEIGHT:
439 pounds

FINAL DRIVE:
Chain

OWNER:
Rex Barrett

Above: Engine was rather flaccid at lower revs, making the RZ a chore to drive in town, but roared to life as it neared its 10,000-rpm redline. *Below:* Fiberglass bodywork hides the unusual V-4, twin-crank, two-stroke engine. Six-speed transmission allowed rider to keep the peaky two-stroke within its narrow—but very high—power range. *Left:* Adjustable anti-dive mechanism on the forks was triggered by application of the front brakes.

1986
DUCATI MONTJUICH

Ducati entered the motorcycle market with small displacement, single-cylinder machines. Designer Fabio Taglioni arrived in the mid-Fifties, adding a shaft-driven overhead cam and desmodromic valve actuation to Ducati's racing engines. By 1971, both these features were available on the company's road-going models, and single-cylinder Ducatis in 250-, 350-, and 450-cc sizes were potent machines.

Venturing into the Sportbike market in 1971, Ducati introduced a 750-cc V-twin with the traditional shaft-driven cams and desmodromic valve gear. It was followed by larger-displacement versions, and the V-twin engine remains a Ducati trademark today. But there was a time when it appeared as though the Italian company with its famous "desmo" engines was on its last legs. Luckily for Sportbike enthusiasts, Cagiva entered the picture and rescued the Ducati name from the brink of disaster.

To develop the Montjuich, Cagiva management lured Fabio Taglioni out of retirement to breathe new life into the tired 90-degree V-twin engine. Having done so, Ducati assembled the rest of the motorcycle—sparing no expense—for racing homologation. Only 200 of the 750-cc bikes were built, a mere 10 finding their way to the U.S.

YEAR:
1986

MANUFACTURER:
Ducati

MODEL:
Montjuich

ENGINE TYPE:
V-twin

DISPLACEMENT:
748 cc (approx. 45 cubic inches)

VALVE TRAIN:
Overhead cam with desmodromic valve actuation

CARBURETION:
Dell'Orto

TRANSMISSION:
Five-speed, foot shift

FRONT SUSPENSION:
Telescopic

FRONT BRAKE(S):
Dual discs

REAR SUSPENSION:
Swingarm with coil-over shock

REAR BRAKE:
Disc

WEIGHT:
367 pounds

FINAL DRIVE:
Chain

OWNER:
Matt Jonas

The Montjuich (pronounced mont-ju-EEK) is one of the rarest of Ducatis—which are pretty rare in the U.S. anyway. *Above:* Up front, dual Brembo floating discs with drilled rotors provided strong stopping power. *Bottom:* Ducati's 90-degree V-twin has sometimes been referred to as an "L-twin," because the rear cylinder points almost straight up and the front cylinder almost straight forward.

1986
SUZUKI RG 500

The RG 500 Gamma was built to defend Suzuki's honor against Yamaha's new RZ 500. Though both were technical marvels, they were answers to a question no one was asking.

Being extremely light and driven by a potent two-stroke powerplant, the Gamma is a loose cannon, with a high, narrow powerband and a throttle best described as a light switch. Around town, the RG is docile and handles well, but spinning the tach into the upper reaches brings a whole new meaning to the word "peaky." An experienced rider on the proper roads will find the Gamma capable of tremendous speeds, but a novice will seldom be able to tap the potential.

Construction of the Gamma centers around an all-aluminum, box-section chassis. The engine is a two-stroke "square four" with two crankshafts, providing the pilot with 90 horsepower. With a dry weight of 340 pounds, the Gamma was almost fifty pounds lighter than its competition from Yamaha.

In the end, both Suzuki and Yamaha had overestimated the demand for a street-legal race bike and sales figures languished. Although never imported directly into the United States, a handful of Gammas found their way in from across the Canadian border.

YEAR:
1986

MANUFACTURER:
Suzuki

MODEL:
RG 500

ENGINE TYPE:
Square four with dual crank-shafts

DISPLACEMENT:
498 cc (approx. 30 cubic inches)

VALVE TRAIN:
Two-stroke

CARBURETION:
Mikuni

TRANSMISSION:
Six-speed, foot shift

FRONT SUSPENSION:
Telescopic

FRONT BRAKE(S):
Dual discs

REAR SUSPENSION:
Swingarm with coil-over shock

REAR BRAKE:
Disc

WEIGHT:
340 pounds

FINAL DRIVE:
Chain

OWNER:
Rex Barrett

The Gamma's race-bike nature proved a bit high-strung for practical street use, and combined with high prices, resulted in very limited sales. *Opposite page, above, and left:* Each of the four cylinders exhausted through its own muffler; two in the traditional location on each side of the bike, and two out the top, flanking the taillight. *Far left:* Gauges are prominently displayed, with the tach taking center stage.

1988
LAVERDA SFC 1000

Laverda and exoticar-maker Lamborghini share a common trait besides their Italian heritage; both companies built farm implements before producing road-going machines.

Laverda's first motorcycle was a small, single-cylinder bike intended to test the waters of the market. It proved a raging success, and thus began the company's foray into motorcycle manufacturing.

At first, single-cylinder bikes were all Laverda produced. Then in the late Sixties the company ventured a vertical twin, considered quite a risk at the time. It wasn't until 1972 that triples were offered, and it is these for which Laverda is best known.

This SFC 1000 sport-touring model features a 981-cc engine that has amassed an enviable record in racing over the years. Marzoccki suspension at both ends combines a comfortable ride with capable handling, while a trio of disc brakes along with an anti-dive compensator fitted to the front forks insure safe, controlled stops.

Because it was not intended for export, the SFC is a rare sight on U.S. roads. Yet in many respects it is better suited to American tastes than many of the exotic machines that find their way to these shores.

YEAR:
1988

MANUFACTURER:
Laverda

MODEL:
SFC 1000

ENGINE TYPE:
Inline three

DISPLACEMENT:
981 cc (approx. 60 cubic inches)

VALVE TRAIN:
Overhead cam

CARBURETION:
Dell'Orto

TRANSMISSION:
Five-speed, foot shift

FRONT SUSPENSION:
Telescopic

FRONT BRAKE(S):
Dual discs

REAR SUSPENSION:
Swingarm with coil-over shocks

REAR BRAKE:
Disc

WEIGHT:
497 pounds

FINAL DRIVE:
Chain

OWNER:
Matt Jonas

Laverda's three-cylinder engines were initially fitted with single-plane crankshafts that produced uneven firing intervals and an ungainly exhaust note. Later the crankshaft received staggered throws, which resulted in a smoother cadence and more power as well. Gold-painted frame, suspension components, and wheels are classy touches.

1990
BMW K-1

Clad in futuristic plastic bodywork from stem to stern, the BMW K-1 looks more like a design study than a production model from the Black Forest. Based on the "Racer" design mockup done by BMW in 1984, the K-1 represented BMW's desire to appeal to a more youthful market.

The mechanicals found beneath the seven-piece skin are also a departure from BMW's standard fare. A water-cooled, sixteen-valve, inline four-cylinder engine propels the K-1 to a top speed of nearly 150 miles per hour. Final drive is handled by BMW's usual shaft drive, which is housed within the massive, bright yellow, single-sided swingarm. In the front, four-piston calipers grip dual floating rotors. The rear wheel has its own disc brake and both are controlled by an ABS system to ensure safe stops even under less-than-ideal braking conditions.

Intended to compete in the Sport-Touring segment of the market, the K-1 is blessed with a comfortable seating area. The tail section of the bodywork can be removed to expose the passenger's pillion hiding below. Small storage compartments reside on each side of the tail piece, and each one has its own locking cover.

Through the 1980s, BMWs had been unique in design but conservative in execution. With bikes like the K-1 ringing in the '90s, its hard to tell what roads future BMWs will follow.

YEAR:
1990

MANUFACTURER:
BMW

MODEL:
K-1

ENGINE TYPE:
Inline four

DISPLACEMENT:
987 cc (approx. 60 cubic inches)

VALVE TRAIN:
Double overhead cams

CARBURETION:
Fuel injection

TRANSMISSION:
Five-speed, foot shift

FRONT SUSPENSION:
Telescopic

FRONT BRAKE(S):
Dual discs with ABS

REAR SUSPENSION:
Single-side swingarm with coil-over shock

REAR BRAKE:
Disc with ABS

WEIGHT:
569 pounds

FINAL DRIVE:
Shaft

OWNER:
Steve Mitleider

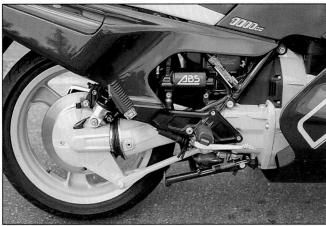

Above: In a sleek departure from normally conservative BMW practice, the K-1 featured a full-enclosure fairing; even the turn signals were faired in, both front and rear. "Toothed" trigger wheels for the anti-lock brake system ride inside the brake rotors; in front, the ABS sensor can be seen beneath the lower edge of the front fender. *Left:* Single-sided swingarm incorporates a U-joint for the differential and a trailing arm to help position the wheel.

1990
HONDA RC30

To the casual observer, the RC30 appears to be just another player in the current crop of fiberglass-bodied Sportbikes. But to those in the know, it is nothing short of a thinly disguised racing machine.

First released to the Japanese market in the late 1980s, American enthusiasts had to wait until 1990 to get their hands on an RC30. Even then, a lofty price and limited availability made them a rare sight on public roads.

Though the 750-cc double-overhead-cam V-4 engine produces "just" 86 horsepower—not a class-leading performance by 1990—it contains race-inspired components such as titanium connecting rods that reduce reciprocating weight. Out front, the wheel and brake pads have quick-release mountings that smack of racing influence. Likewise, the rear wheel, which carries a disc brake to the inside and a chain sprocket to the outside of a single-sided swingarm and attaches with a single lug nut.

Yes, the RC30 may look like just another sports machine, but as we all know, looks can be deceiving.

YEAR:
1990

MANUFACTURER:
Honda

MODEL:
RC30

ENGINE TYPE:
V-four

DISPLACEMENT:
750 cc (approx. 45 cubic inches)

VALVE TRAIN:
Double overhead cams

CARBURETION:
Keihin

TRANSMISSION:
Six-speed, foot shift

FRONT SUSPENSION:
Telescopic

FRONT BRAKE(S):
Dual discs

REAR SUSPENSION:
Single-sided swingarm with coil-over gas shock

REAR BRAKE:
Disc

WEIGHT:
475 pounds

FINAL DRIVE:
Chain

OWNER:
Matt Jonas

The RC30's engine was fairly tame by Sportbike standards, yet this high-revving 750-cc V-4 didn't redline until 12,500 rpm. At 475 pounds, the RC30 was no lightweight, but much of the componentry that contributed to that heft was strongly influenced by Honda's factory racers—and looked it.

1993
BIMOTA DIECI

Italy's reputation for exotic transportation is well known, and amongst the builders of four-wheeled esoterica lies the Bimota facility. Situated on the Adriatic coastline, the city of Rimini is the home of the Dieci, Bimota's latest creation.

Since 1973, Bimota has been handcrafting some of the world's most beautiful motorcycles. By installing powerplants built by other manufacturers, Bimota is able to focus its energy on form and function.

Witness the Dieci. Powered by a Yamaha FZR 1000 engine, this Italian beauty sports a hand-laid fiberglass body surrounding an aluminum frame welded by expert artisans. There are no extraneous brackets or clutter, and each machined component appears to be the work of a gifted sculptor. The stout "upside-down" forks carry Brembo calipers embracing huge floating brake discs that are themselves works of art.

As is often the case, however, the price of excellence is high, and as earlier models began to escalate in cost, Bimota sales showed signs of distress and the company flirted with disaster. Salvation came in the form of the Ducati-powered DB1 introduced in 1986, and today Bimota continues to produce the two-wheeled exotica for which it is known the world over.

YEAR:
1993

MANUFACTURER:
Bimota

MODEL:
Dieci

ENGINE TYPE:
Inline four

DISPLACEMENT:
1000 cc (approx. 61 cubic inches)

VALVE TRAIN:
Double overhead cams

CARBURETION:
NA

TRANSMISSION:
Five speed, foot shift

FRONT SUSPENSION:
Upside-down telescopic

FRONT BRAKE(S):
Dual discs

REAR SUSPENSION:
Swingarm with coil-over shock

REAR BRAKE:
Disc

WEIGHT:
470 pounds

FINAL DRIVE:
Chain

OWNER:
Glen Nesnevich

Futuristic styling and smooth bodywork make the Dieci appear to be milled from a single piece of alloy. Though not as exotic as some powerplants, the 1000-cc Yamaha engine hidden within provides ample power—and can't be seen anyway. *Left:* Dual halogen headlamps light the way, and turn signals are mounted flush with the fairing.

1993
DUCATI SUPERLIGHT

Any Ducati is a rare sight on American roads, partly because their assembly process is largely done by hand. But the 900SS SL Superlight will be particularly scarce, as a total of only 300 were produced.

As unique as the Superlight is, the components used in its construction are not all that exotic—at least for Ducati. Based on the 900SS SP model, the Superlight is first dressed in a coat of Fly Yellow paint—a radical departure from the traditional Ducati red. Complimenting the sporting paint treatment is a solo seat, which dispels any notions of two-up riding.

In the hardware department, the Superlight has a stock 900SS SP powerplant decked out in carbon fiber regalia. Almost every non-structural cover on the engine has been replaced with a carbon fiber version to trim excess bulk. Even the upswept twin exhaust canisters are formed in carbon fiber in an effort to trim every possible ounce from the Superlight's fighting weight.

YEAR:
1993

MANUFACTURER:
Ducati

MODEL:
Superlight

ENGINE TYPE:
V-twin

DISPLACEMENT:
904 cc (approx. 55 cubic inches)

VALVE TRAIN:
Overhead cam with desmodromic valve actuation

CARBURETION:
Mikuni

TRANSMISSION:
Six-speed, foot shift

FRONT SUSPENSION:
Telescopic

FRONT BRAKE(S):
Dual discs

REAR SUSPENSION:
Single-sided swingarm with coil-over shock

REAR BRAKE:
Disc

WEIGHT:
390 pounds

FINAL DRIVE:
Chain

OWNER:
Motorcycle Center

Opposite page: Barely visible behind the Superlight's enveloping fairing is its 904-cc "Pantah" V-twin. Since 1985, Ducati's Pantah engines have used cogged belts to drive the overhead cams rather than the traditional (for Ducati) shaft with bevel gears. Those engines also use a dry clutch as opposed to the usual wet clutch, which runs in an oil bath. *This page, top:* The Marvic 3-spoke alloy wheels, enormous front brake rotors, and wide tires add to the race-bike theme. *Above left:* Decal on tach warns riders not to exceed the 9000-rpm redline. *Above right:* To further signify its exclusivity, each Superlight wears a numbered plaque.

1994
BMW R1100RSL

The R1100RSL is the result of over 70 years of Teutonic engineering. And though BMW has since adopted inline threes and fours for some of its machines, its horizontally opposed "boxer" engine was for years synonymous with the company's name.

The RSL is rife with changes from earlier models. Both the fuel delivery and the three-way, closed-loop catalytic converter are controlled by an on-board microcomputer that would humble many PCs. To insure mechanical integrity, each of the connecting rods is cracked into two halves around the main boss during production to leave a "unique fracture surface" that provides a perfect alignment upon reassembly.

Front and rear wheels are managed with a suspension system that is unique to BMW. The Telelever front end consists of a telescopic fork that is sprung with a single shock and provides the latest in comfort and handling. The single-sided swingarm houses the drive shaft and is controlled by a gas-filled shock.

YEAR:
1994

MANUFACTURER:
BMW

MODEL:
R1100RSL

ENGINE TYPE:
Horizontally opposed twin

DISPLACEMENT:
1092 cc (approx. 66 cubic inches)

VALVE TRAIN:
Overhead valves

CARBURETION:
Bosch fuel injection

TRANSMISSION:
Five-speed, foot shift

FRONT SUSPENSION:
Telelever

FRONT BRAKE(S):
Dual discs

REAR SUSPENSION:
Single-sided swingarm with coil-over shock

REAR BRAKE:
Disc

WEIGHT:
527 pounds

FINAL DRIVE:
Shaft

OWNER:
Laurel BMW Motorcycles

Top left: R1100RSL retained BMW's traditional "boxer" two-cylinder engine, but gained four-valve heads for more power. *Top right:* Anti-lock brakes were optional, and the bike featured is so equipped. What looks like a ring of gear teeth around the inside of the brake disc is the trigger wheel that relays wheel speed to the ABS sensor. *Bottom:* Exhaust pipes join behind the front wheel, wrap around to the right side of the bike, and exit to a muffler on the left side *(opposite page)*.

231

1994
BUELL S2 THUNDERBOLT

By combining the latest hardware from Buell with the financial backing of Harley-Davidson, the S2 Thunderbolt is poised to make a full-scale attack on the popular Sportbike market.

Eric Buell is certainly no amateur when it comes to performance motorcycles, as he has been designing and building Harley-powered Sportbikes for some time. In the past, however, production rarely exceeded 100 units per year; with Harley-Davidson as a 49-percent partner, annual sales are now expected to number in the thousands.

Powering the S2 is a modified 1203-cc V-twin from the Harley-Davidson Sportster. Each of the space-age frames are built by hand from chrome-moly tubing. Out front is a huge 13-inch brake rotor gripped by a six-piston Brembo caliper, while in back an aluminum swingarm activates an extension coil-over shock mounted beneath the engine.

The combination of a low center of gravity, sophisticated suspension, and a compact 55-inch wheelbase insures that the Buell S2 Thunderbolt handles like no other Harley-powered bike before it. And the Sportster-based engine insures that it sounds like no other Sportbike on the road.

YEAR:
1994

MANUFACTURER:
Buell

MODEL:
S2 Thunderbolt

ENGINE TYPE:
V-twin

DISPLACEMENT:
1203 cc (approx. 74 cubic inches)

VALVE TRAIN:
Overhead valves

CARBURETION:
NA

TRANSMISSION:
Five-speed, foot shift

FRONT SUSPENSION:
Telescopic

FRONT BRAKE(S):
Disc

REAR SUSPENSION:
Swingarm with coil-over shock

REAR BRAKE:
Disc

WEIGHT:
450 pounds

FINAL DRIVE:
Belt

OWNER:
Illinois Harley-Davidson

Opposite page: Harley-Davidson tried marketing its own sports-oriented motorcycle back in 1977, but the XLCR wasn't well received—primarily because it couldn't match the performance of Japanese rivals. The S2, which boasts Buell's latest technical refinements, promises to be a true contender. Note that canister muffler mounted under the bike exhausts unceremoniously in front of the rear wheel. *Far left and below:* Adjustable rear shock also mounts beneath the bike. Unlike most sporting machines, power is transferred to the rear wheel via cogged belt. *Left:* Taillight is flanked by decorative grilles.

233

1994
DUCATI 916

Late in the 1994 model year, Ducati unleashed a new warrior into the Superbike arena. After chalking up numerous victories on racetracks around the world, the 916 set out to make its mark on the street.

Though its engine spotted two cylinders and 100 ccs to most liter-class competitors, the 916 was a serious threat to Japanese rivals. Displacing 916 ccs and boasting an 11:1 compression ratio, Ducati's traditional V-twin with unique desmodromic valve actuation pumped 105 horsepower to the rear wheel. While that hardly made the 916 the most powerful bike in its class, a combination of composite materials, compact design, and weight-saving engineering certainly made it one of the lightest; at 438 pounds, the 916 could best be described as svelte.

With just 400 planned for exportation to the U.S., the 916 promises to be a rare sight on American roads. But those fortunate enough to snare one will be rewarded with a most graceful and exotic expression of a state-of-the-art Superbike—Italian style.

YEAR:
1994

MANUFACTURER:
Ducati

MODEL:
916

ENGINE TYPE:
V-twin

DISPLACEMENT:
916 cc (Approx. 56 cubic inches)

VALVE TRAIN:
Double overhead cams with desmodromic valve actuation

CARBURETION:
Fuel injection

TRANSMISSION:
Six-speed, foot shift

FRONT SUSPENSION:
Telescopic

FRONT BRAKE(S):
Dual discs

REAR SUSPENSION:
Single-sided swingarm with coil-over shock

REAR BRAKE:
Disc

WEIGHT:
438 pounds

FINAL DRIVE:
Chain

OWNER:
Bollenbach Engineering

Opposite page: Unlike most other Ducatis, the 916 uses a water-cooled, twin-cam version of the traditional desmodromic V-twin. *Above:* Engine exhausts through mufflers mounted beneath the tail fairing. *Left:* Copper-colored cylinder behind fork brace is a steering stabilizer that helps reduce the bike's "twitchiness."

1995
HARLEY-DAVIDSON FXSTSB

Harley's latest custom is dubbed the "Bad Boy." Powered by the company's big 80-cubic-inch V-twin, it carries a modernized version of the springer front forks used on early Harleys up through the Forties.

Virtually all frame and body components are cloaked in black, from the front forks (typically chromed) to the rear license-plate bracket. Coal black covers the frame, fenders, oil tank, and fuel tank, the last carrying a metal badge in place of the usual printed graphics.

Lest you fear the Bad Boy treatment is all for show, Harley has married the retro styling treatment to a host of contemporary mechanical features. A multi-link arrangement on the front forks allows the fender to hug the 21-inch tire more closely than in the past, and the "softtail" rear suspension looks rigid but isn't. The V-twin's prodigious torque is transferred to the cast rear wheel via modern belt drive, and dual disc brakes utilizing semi-floating calipers help haul the Bad Boy's 633-pound heft to a stop—so everyone can get a better look.

YEAR:
1995

MANUFACTURER:
Harley-Davidson

MODEL:
FXSTSB

ENGINE TYPE:
V-twin

DISPLACEMENT:
80 cubic inches

VALVE TRAIN:
Overhead valves

CARBURETION:
Keihin

TRANSMISSION:
Five-speed, foot shift

FRONT SUSPENSION:
Leading link with coil springs and hydraulic shock

FRONT BRAKE(S):
Disc

REAR SUSPENSION:
Triangulated swingarm with coil-over shock

REAR BRAKE:
Disc

WEIGHT:
633 pounds

FINAL DRIVE:
Belt

OWNER:
Heritage Harley-Davidson

Left and below: Though subtlety would not seem to be in the Bad Boy's vocabulary, it boasts several fine styling touches: "Bad Boy" lettering on the air cleaner cover; blackout speedometer nacelle; highway pegs with high-mounted brake pedal; and spear-shaped graphic on the front fender.

INDEX